NATIONS *IN TRANSITION*

NORTH KOREA

by Debra A. Miller

GREENHAVEN
PRESS®

THOMSON
™
GALE

San Diego • Detroit • New York • San Francisco • Cleveland
New Haven, Conn. • Waterville, Maine • London • Munich

© 2004 by Greenhaven Press. Greenhaven Press is an imprint of The Gale Group, Inc., a division of Thomson Learning, Inc.

Greenhaven® and Thomson Learning™ are trademarks used herein under license.

For more information, contact
Greenhaven Press
27500 Drake Rd.
Farmington Hills, MI 48331-3535
Or you can visit our Internet site at http://www.gale.com

LIBRARY OF CONGRESS CATALOGING-IN-PUBLICATION DATA

North Korea / Debra A. Miller, book author
   p. cm. — (Nations in transition)
Includes bibiliographical references and index.
Summary: Examines the history of North Korea from its creation during the Cold War to the present, the challenges faced by the country following the collapse of communism, its development of nuclear weapons, and North Korea's place in the world today.
   ISBN 0-7377-1098-5 (lib.: alk. paper)
   1. Korea (North) 2. Nuclear weapons—Korea (North) I. Miller, Debra A. II. Series.
DS932.N64 2004
951.9304'3—dc21

                                                                2003048326

Printed in the United States of America

Contents

Foreword

In 1986 Soviet general secretary Mikhail Gorbachev initiated his plan to reform the economic, political, and social structure of the Soviet Union. Nearly three-quarters of a century of Communist ideology was dismantled in the next five years. As the totalitarian regime relaxed its rule and opened itself up to the West, the Soviet peoples clamored for more freedoms. Hard-line Communists resisted Gorbachev's lead, but glasnost, or "openness," could not be stopped with the will of the common people behind it.

In 1991 the changing USSR held its first multicandidate elections. The reform-minded Boris Yeltsin, a supporter of Gorbachev, became the first popularly elected president of the Russian Republic in Soviet history. Under Yeltsin's leadership, the old Communist policies soon all but disintegrated, as did the Soviet Union itself. The Union of Soviet Socialist Republics broke apart into fifteen independent entities. The former republics reformed into a more democratic union now referred to as the Commonwealth of Independent States. Russia remained the nominal figurehead of the commonwealth, but it no longer dictated the future of the other independent states.

By the new millennium, Russia and the other commonwealth states still faced crises. The new states were all in transition from decades of totalitarian rule to the postglasnost era of unprecedented and untested democratic reforms. Revamping the Soviet economy may have opened up new opportunities in private ownership of property and business, but it did not bring overnight prosperity to the former republics. Common necessities such as food still remain in short supply in many regions. And while new governments seek to stabilize their authority, crime rates have escalated throughout the former Soviet Union. Still, the people are confident that their newfound freedoms—freedom of speech and assembly, freedom of religion, and even the right of workers to strike—will ultimately better their lives. The process of change will take time and the people are willing to see their respective states through the challenges of this transitional period in Soviet history.

The collapse and rebuilding of the former Soviet Union provides perhaps the best example of a contemporary "nation in transition," the focus of this Greenhaven Press series. However, other nations that fall under the series rubric have faced a host of unique and varied cultural shifts. India, for instance, is a stable, guiding force in Asia, yet it remains a nation in transition more than fifty years after winning independence from Great Britain. The entire infrastructure of the Indian subcontinent still bears the marking of its colonial past: In a land of eighteen official spoken languages, for example, English remains the voice of politics and education. India is still coming to grips with its colonial legacy while forging its place as a strong player in Asian and world affairs.

North Korea's place in Greenhaven's Nations in Transition series is based on major recent political developments. After decades of antagonism between its Communist government and the democratic leadership of South Korea, tensions seemed to ease in the late 1990s. Even under the shadow of the North's developing nuclear capabilities, the presidents of both North and South Korea met in 2000 to propose plans for possible reunification of the two estranged nations. And though it is one of the three remaining bastions of communism in the world, North Korea is choosing not to remain an isolated relic of the Cold War. While it has not earned the trust of the United States and many of its Western allies, North Korea has begun to reach out to its Asian neighbors to encourage trade and cultural exchanges.

These three countries exemplify the types of changes and challenges that qualify them as subjects of study in the Greenhaven Nations in Transition series. The series examines specific nations to disclose the major social, political, economic, and cultural shifts that have caused massive change and in many cases, brought about regional and/or worldwide shifts in power. Detailed maps, inserts, and pictures help flesh out the people, places, and events that define the country's transitional period. Furthermore, a comprehensive bibliography points readers to other sources that will deepen their understanding of the nation's complex past and contemporary struggles. With these tools, students and casual readers trace both past history and future challenges of these important nations.

Introduction
The Cold War Conundrum

In a speech delivered in January 2002, U.S. president George W. Bush characterized North Korea as a country that threatens the peace of the world by supporting terrorism and developing weapons of mass destruction. North Korea objected to Bush's characterization, but in October 2002 North Korea admitted that it was developing nuclear weapons and possibly chemical and biological weapons as well. North Korea's admission placed it on the front page of newspapers around the world and increased worries about nuclear weapons proliferation. North Korea's announcement also imparted urgency to the debate about how to solve the conundrum of North Korea—an isolated and starving, yet highly militarized and aggressive, relic of the Cold War, led by one of the few remaining Communist regimes in the world.

Created in 1948 as a Soviet-sponsored country called the Democratic People's Republic of Korea (DPRK), North Korea quickly showed its inclination toward militarism by invading South Korea in 1950. The invasion was an attempt to reunify Korea under Communist leadership following a division of the peninsula by the Soviet Union and the United States at the end of World War II. The resulting Korean War raged for three years, but did not result in the reunification of Korea. Instead, it ushered in more than five decades of hostilities between North and South Korea.

After the war against its neighbor, North Korea retreated into isolation for many decades under the repressive leadership of Kim Il Sung, who created a cult of personality around himself modeled on that of Soviet Union leader Joseph Stalin. During this time North Korea developed as a Communist-led state that relied on massive economic support and military protection from the Soviet Union and China.

At the same time, however, Kim Il Sung emphasized national independence and self-sufficiency. He conducted an ongoing guerrilla war against South Korea designed to destabilize the South Korean government and lead to the long-desired Korean unity. To further this goal Kim devoted much of his nation's resources to the military, in the process developing the world's fifth-largest armed force.

With the end of the Cold War and the collapse of the Soviet Union in 1991, North Korea lost its largest benefactor. Without Soviet economic aid and protection, the country quickly went into dramatic economic decline. Communist China, North Korea's other main supporter, was focused on instituting its own economic and free-market reforms and was unable to make up for the shortfall. In the mid-1990s, natural disasters, including floods and droughts, exacerbated the nation's problems by reducing food production. Mass starvation and malnutrition resulted. To survive, North Korea begged for aid in

Two Korean children pose in front of a tank during the Korean War. The war began in 1950 when North Korea invaded South Korea.

North Koreans pay homage to a statue of Kim Il Sung in Pyongyang.

the form of food from the United Nations. To earn badly needed cash, it sold missiles and arms to other nations, such as Iran, Iraq, and Syria.

North Korea was also forced by its adversity to seek engagement with its former enemies—South Korea, the United States, and Japan. To the outside world, however, the government's policies, first under Kim Il Sung and then under his son, Kim Jong Il, appeared erratic and militant. North Korea's foreign policy included diplomatic overtures, such as a historic summit meeting in 2000 with South Korean president Kim Dae Jung, but also military actions and nuclear threats, which it appeared to use as leverage to force negotiations and reach its goals—a foreign policy many have described as brinksmanship or nuclear blackmail.

For example, in 1993 North Korea precipitated a crisis by refusing to allow international inspections of its nuclear facilities after evidence was found that it was working to develop nuclear weapons in violation of treaties it had signed. Talks with the United States defused the crisis and resulted in an agreement under which North Korea agreed to end its nuclear weapons program in exchange for fuel oil and aid in building light-water reactors for electrical production. Similarly, in 1998 North Korea test-fired an intermediate-range missile over Japan, causing international alarm. After the United

States agreed to a dialogue, North Korea suspended its missile testing in exchange for promises that U.S. economic sanctions would be lifted.

Although North Korea in the October 2002 incident asked not for economic benefits but for a nonaggression treaty with the United States, the latest crisis appeared to many to be another of the country's gambits designed to engage the United States in talks and achieve the North Korean goals of gaining foreign aid and security through negotiations. Other analysts say that North Korea's historic militaristic approach (and its recent moves toward acquisition of nuclear weapons) are logical from the perspective of a small and poor nation run by a regime that fears losing control and is concerned about a military invasion or takeover by more powerful countries. Indeed, these experts view North Korea as a textbook example of how a small country can wield power in a nuclear world. In any case, North Korea's foreign policy clearly has been successful to date from the standpoint of enabling Kim Jong Il's regime to survive unchallenged long after the fall of communism in many nations around the world.

At the beginning of the twenty-first century, North Korea is at a critical turning point in its history. Its challenge is to overcome its Cold War legacy—a repressive government and a failing state-run economy—and to find a new place in the international community. So far, the ruling regime has shown a reluctance to embrace bold economic reform or shed North Korea's isolation, instead using military leverage to help it meet minimal survival needs and stay in power. Whether Kim Jong Il's policies will lead North Korea into a peaceful relationship with other nations or into discord and possible military conflict remains to be seen. What can be said at this point is that North Korea truly is a nation in transition.

North Korea's Beginnings: The Cold War Division of Korea 1

Throughout their history, the people of Korea resisted numerous invasions by foreign powers, including repeated attempts by China to dominate the Korean peninsula. This aggression from neighboring countries fostered a fierce determination among Koreans to be free from foreign rule, and they eventually formed a united and independent Korean kingdom that endured for many centuries. This long period of independence, however, came to an end when imperial Japan colonized Korea in 1910. Eventually, the Japanese were expelled, but Koreans' desire for independence and unity was thwarted again in 1945 as Korea became a pawn in the ideological conflict between the United States and the Soviet Union known as the Cold War.

The Roots of Communism on the Korean Peninsula

Modern North Korea occupies the northern part of the Korean peninsula, where it is surrounded by more powerful nations. China and Russia both share borders with North Korea, and Japan lies just across the Sea of Japan. In large part, Korea's geography has determined its destiny; throughout its long history, Korea was subject to invasion and subjugation by its more powerful neighbors. As journalist Don Oberdorfer points out, "Korea has suffered nine hundred invasions, great and small, in its two thousand years of recorded history."[1]

Korea's early history, for example, includes multiple invasions by the Chinese. The Chinese invaded and conquered the ancient Korean kingdom of Choson as early as 108 B.C., establishing four Chinese-controlled colonies. Koreans resisted the Chinese control, and after many centuries the Korean people slowly coalesced into three separate and independent Korean kingdoms—Koguryo, Paekche, and Silla. All three kingdoms, however, had to repel repeated Chinese invasions. At the same time, these three kingdoms warred with each other. Silla eventually defeated and subsumed both Paekche and Koguryo, ousted Chinese invasion forces that by then had taken over Koguryo, and by the end of the seventh century formed the first united Korean government. The kingdom of Silla fell in 935 due to internal problems, and it was followed by the kingdom of Koryo until it, in turn, was weakened by Mongol invasions and Japanese raids.

Eventually Korea entered a 518-year period of prosperity under the Yi or Choson dynasty, named after ancient Choson and founded by General Yi Song-gye in 1392. During this time Korea became known as the "Hermit Kingdom," because it adopted a policy of isolating itself from almost all foreign influence. This isolation was broken in the sixteenth century by Japanese invasions, which were repelled after Korea requested the assistance of the Chinese, and by a Chinese Manchurian invasion in the early 1600s. These interruptions, however, were followed by another two centuries of peace. Unfortunately for Korea, this long history of unity and independence ended when Japan annexed Korea in 1910, making it a Japanese colony.

Japanese influence in Korea had begun in 1875, when Japan used its warships to force Korea to open itself to Japanese and Western trade. Meanwhile, China also was seeking influence in Korea. Eventually, competition between Japan and China over Korea led to war. Japan defeated the Chinese and under the terms of the 1895 Treaty of Shimonoseki that ended the war, the Chinese agreed to end their involvement in

Korean affairs, setting the stage for future Japanese exploitation of the peninsula.

After the Japanese victory over China, Russia established its own sphere of dominance in Korea, and France and Germany sided with Russia to oppose Japan's influence. In 1904 the rivalry between Japan and Russia finally erupted into war, culminating in another treaty after Russia's defeat, the 1905 Treaty of Portsmouth. Under this agreement Russia recognized Japan's right to control the Korean peninsula. This treaty was mediated by the United States, which fully condoned the Japanese takeover of Korea in exchange for assurances that Japan would not oppose U.S. dominance of the Philippines. Finally, in 1910 Japan formally annexed Korea, and Korea became a Japanese colony for the next four decades.

Once again, the Korean people, having fought against Chinese domination and control for centuries, found themselves living under foreign rule. The Japanese imposed a brutal military regime that used violence to subjugate the Korean people and exploit Korea's resources. The Japanese, for example, confiscated Korean land and property through an ambitious land survey. The survey required Koreans to prove their land ownership; those who could not show clear title saw their property confiscated and awarded to Japanese companies or individuals. Because most Korean lands historically were controlled by royal families and worked by peasants or owned communally by villages or whole families, with no clear records concerning who held title, the Japanese land survey left most Koreans homeless and in poverty. The Japanese also treated native Koreans as their cultural inferiors and forced them to adopt Japanese dress and customs, and even to fight in the Japanese military.

Just as they had in the case of Chinese invaders, Koreans resisted the Japanese colonizers. On March 1, 1919, soon after the completion of the land survey, the first eruption of Korean resistance to Japanese rule occured as Koreans from all levels of society demonstrated for independence in what became known as the March First Movement. The resistance began as an independence declaration signed by prominent Korean landowners, intellectuals, religious leaders, and others. The declaration called for peaceful public demonstrations and appeals to foreign powers for assistance in achieving Korean independence. Thereafter, demonstrators in towns across Korea assembled to read the declaration and shout their support for independence. As historian Takashi Hatada describes,

> Throughout the nation people joined the movement and took part in the mass parades—old men, young men, women, and children of all classes. In March and April, when the movement was at its height, it is estimated that about 500,000 people actively joined in the demonstrations, and the members

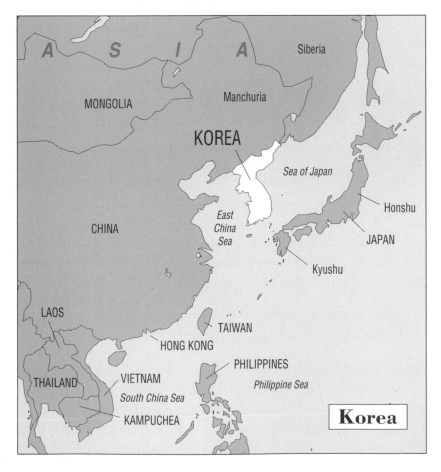

The March First Movement

The Japanese annexed Korea in 1910. A series of protests against the Japanese began throughout Korea in 1919; these came to be known as the March First Movement, the beginning of Korean resistance to Japanese occupation and colonization of Korea. The movement began within the context of U.S. president Woodrow Wilson's doctrine of national self-determination and Russia's Bolshevik revolution, both of which inspired Koreans to overcome their oppression and strive for independence in Korea. On March 1, 1919, a declaration of independence was signed by thirty-three prominent Koreans. As quoted by Geoff Simons in his book, *Korea: The Search for Sovereignty*, the declaration of independence stated:

> We herewith proclaim the independence of Korea and the liberty of the Korean people. We tell it to the world in witness of the equality of all nations and we pass it on to our posterity as their inherent right. We make this proclamation, having back of us five thousand years of history and twenty millions of a united loyal people. We take this step to insure to our children, for all time to come, personal liberty in accord with the awakening consciousness of this new era. This is the clear leading of God, the moving principle of the present age, the whole human race's just claim. It is something that cannot be stamped out, or stifled, or gagged, or suppressed by any means.

The March First Movement urged not armed struggle but peaceful protests and calls for assistance from foreign governments. It resulted in mass demonstrations throughout Korea, which were reported worldwide. Ultimately, however, the Japanese repressed the resistance movement with force, arresting, wounding, and in many cases, killing Korean demonstrators.

of the movement numbered over a million. All over Korea resounded the cry: "Long live independence."[2]

When foreign support did not materialize the Japanese quickly and ruthlessly suppressed the demonstrations. The resistance movement, however, inspired great feelings of nationalism in Korea, and thereafter Koreans continued their resistance, both underground within Korea and from exile in China and elsewhere.

Nationalist leaders from the March First Movement established a provisional government in exile, based in Shanghai. Under the leadership of nationalists such as Syngman Rhee, the provisional government developed a constitution, elected officials, and published a newsletter. As exiles, however, these nationalists had little contact with most Koreans; Syngman Rhee, for example, actually lived in the United States during much of this period. In addition, the nationalists were divided about strategy, some factions arguing for armed struggle against the Japanese and others, such as Rhee, convinced that diplomacy would win U.S. support for Korean independence. The provisional government,

Syngman Rhee (center) led a provisional Korean government based in Shanghai during the Japanese occupation of Korea.

therefore, was fragmented and weak, and its activities had little impact on the Japanese occupation of Korea.

Another branch of Korean nationalists that emerged following the independence movement took a more active role in resisting Japanese rule. This was a Communist and Socialist faction that included many organizations of workers, peasants, students, and intellectuals within Korea, as well as exiles living in the Soviet Union and China. Many of these groups identified with the goals of the Bolshevik revolution in Russia, and saw Marxism-Leninism and armed struggle as potential tools for evicting the Japanese from Korea. Unlike the provisional-government nationalists, the Communists focused on the needs of the people by organizing numerous peasant uprisings, student protests, and worker strikes, as well as political protests.

The Communists also tended to be more willing than the nationalists to confront the Japanese militarily. Communist groups in Manchuria, for example, set up paramilitary units and launched effective guerrilla strikes on Japanese military police. As a result of these activities, these Communist guerrillas soon were viewed as heroes by oppressed Koreans. Among the guerrilla fighters in Manchuria at this time was a young man named Kim Il Sung, who helped expand the revolutionary campaign against the Japanese, eventually drawing increased Japanese military raids that forced his withdrawal into exile in the Soviet Union.

Ultimately, the Communists won the hearts and minds of Koreans. Scholar Dae-sook Suh has said that the Communists and their political allies:

> succeeded in wresting control of the Korean revolution from the Nationalists; they planted a deep core of Communist influence among Korean people, particularly the students, youth groups, laborers and peasants. Their fortitude and, at times, obstinate determination to succeed had a profound influence on Korean intellectuals and writers. To the older Koreans, who had groveled so long before seemingly endless foreign suppression, commu-

nism seemed a new hope and a magic touch. . . . For Koreans in general, the sacrifices of the Communists, if not the idea of communism, made strong appeal, far stronger than any occasional bomb-throwing exercise of the Nationalists. The haggard appearance of the Communists suffering from torture, their stern and disciplined attitude toward the common enemy of all Koreans, had a far-reaching effect on people.[3]

The Creation of North Korea

The Japanese were finally ousted from Korea by the Allies at the end of World War II on August 15, 1945. Koreans celebrated Japan's defeat because they believed independence was at hand. These hopes were dashed, however, as Korea once again was occupied by foreign powers.

Notably, both the United States and the Soviet Union had pledged earlier that Korea should become independent after the war; this promise, however, was forgotten in 1945. Instead, the Americans and the Soviets imposed a temporary international trusteeship plan on Korea that called for the creation of an interim Korean government and for elections to be held within five years. In the meantime, the country was divided in half and subjected to a military occupation, with the Soviet Union occupying the area above the thirty-eighth parallel and the United States occupying the zone south of that line.

This new occupation had actually begun when Russian troops entered the northern part of Korea to fight the Japanese shortly before Japan's formal surrender to the Allies at the end of World War II. The Russians were welcomed by Koreans as liberators. As they organized to establish and maintain law and order during the transition from Japanese occupation, the Soviets were assisted by the Korean Communists who had been associated with the anti-Japanese resistance movement. The Soviet Union promised not to interfere in Korean affairs, stating, "The happiness of the Korean people can be achieved only through the efforts and steadfast struggle of the Korean people," and "The Soviet Army has not come to Korea to gain territory or to establish a Soviet system on the Korean territory."[4]

Nevertheless, the Soviets immediately began to dominate the North. To accomplish this, they sought out Korean Communists who were both popular at home and amenable to Soviet influence. They found the perfect combination of those attributes in Kim Il Sung, a hero of the anti-Japanese guerrilla war who had been exiled to the Soviet Union and who had become a member of the Soviet army during his time there. By October 1945 Kim Il Sung was presented by the Russians to North Koreans as their future leader.

Instead of imposing a direct military government on the North, the Soviets and Kim Il Sung worked closely with local Communists and local Korean people's committees to consolidate various factions into a central Communist party and begin the creation of a Communist state. Their efforts met

Demonstrators in Seoul protest the Soviet occupation of North Korea in 1946.

with very little opposition, at least partly because the increasing Soviet control was accompanied by reforms beneficial to Koreans, including a program that distributed land formerly owned by the Japanese and Korean landlords to the peasants. Those who did oppose Soviet actions, such as right-wing nationalists or Koreans who had collaborated with the Japanese, were either expelled from the country or simply executed.

A Widening Gulf

Meanwhile, actions by the United States in southern Korea tended to widen the gulf between North and South. The United States sought to create a democratically elected anti-Communist government in southern Korea. In contrast to the Soviet approach in the North, the United States imposed direct military rule and immediately proclaimed its authority, with U.S. general Douglas MacArthur stating in September 1945, "By virtue of the authority vested in me as Commander in Chief, United States Army Forces, Pacific, I hereby establish military control over Korea south of 38 degrees latitude and the inhabitants thereof. . . . Acts of resistance to the occupying forces or any acts which may disturb public peace and safety will be punished severely. . . . "[5] Not surprisingly, the U.S. occupation inspired strong opposition among many South Koreans. The American approach reminded Koreans of the Japanese occupation; indeed, many Japanese officials were initially permitted by the Americans to remain in power.

Although the United States was committed to the idea of a unified Korea, it was concerned that the majority of those supporting unification and independence were leftists and that a unified Korea might fall under Communist rule. In the South, therefore, the United States suppressed these pro-independent influences and emphasized law and order. It also backed the nationalists who had been part of the provisional government and brought Syngman Rhee, an autocrat and staunch anti-Communist, back to Korea.

With the Soviets ensconced in the North organizing a Communist government and the United States supporting the right-wing nationalists in the South, Korea quickly became divided along ideological lines. Amid this growing ideological split in Korea, talks between the Soviet Union and the United States failed to establish an interim Korean government as called for under the terms of the trusteeship. Finally, the United States abandoned its efforts to negotiate with the Soviets and in August 1947 referred the Korean question to the United Nations (UN), which set up a commission to arrange for and supervise free elections on the peninsula. The Russians, however, believing the process was tainted by U.S. influence over the UN, refused to abide by the UN resolutions and refused to allow the UN commission into North Korea to supervise elections. UN-sponsored elections were therefore held only in South Korea. The result was the creation of an independent Republic of Korea (ROK) on August 15, 1948, with Syngman Rhee as the duly elected president. That same year, Communists in the North, with the Soviets' blessing, created the Democratic People's Republic of Korea (DPRK), headed by Kim Il Sung. Each regime claimed that its was the only legitimate Korean government and both pledged to reunify the Korean peninsula.

The Soviets withdrew their forces from North Korea late in 1948, entrusting the North to the Communist regime they had created. The United States withdrew from South Korea the following year. Both North and South built up their military forces, but the Soviet-supported North, with more forces and better training, held clear military advantage over the much weaker and lesser-prepared South. The North soon was poised to take full advantage of the South's weakness.

The Korean War and Its Legacy

Numerous border clashes followed in the wake of the superpowers' retreat as the ideological conflict between North and South festered, along with an intense desire on both sides for reunification. The tensions on the border escalated into all-out war when North Korea invaded the South with Soviet support on June 25, 1950, in an effort to reunify the Korean peninsula by military means.

Within weeks of the invasion, what began as a civil war became an international conflict, as the United States and the UN came to the defense of the South. On July 7, 1950, the UN authorized a unified UN Command to fight the North Korean invaders, with American general Douglas MacArthur as its leader. By the time the U.S. and UN forces entered the war, North Korea, with its superior military, had already captured Seoul and had pushed southward from there. The North, however, soon found itself on the defensive, as MacArthur staged a dramatic landing behind North Korean lines at the port of Inchon in early September 1950. UN forces retook Seoul shortly thereafter. In the following weeks, the U.S./UN ground

The Demilitarized Zone (DMZ)

When the Korean War ended in 1953 with an armistice agreement instead of a permanent peace treaty, North and South Korea remained hostile neighbors, separated by a two-and-a-half-mile stretch of land along the border called the demilitarized zone, or DMZ. Author Don Oberdorfer describes this area in his book, *The Two Koreas:*

> The demilitarized zone between North and South Korea is bordered by high fences of barbed and razor wire on the north and south, and guarded on the two sides by more than a thousand guard posts, watch towers, and reinforced bunkers across the width of the peninsula. On hair-trigger alert behind the fortifications are two of the world's largest aggregations of military force—1.1 million North Koreans facing 660,000 South Koreans and 37,000 Americans, the latter backed by the full military power of the world's most powerful nation. All sides are heavily armed and ready at a moment's notice to fight another bloody and devastating war. Now that the Berlin wall has fallen and the Soviet Union has collapsed, this pristine nature preserve marks the most dangerous and heavily fortified border in the world. The common wisdom of American GIs on duty in the area is "there ain't no D in the DMZ."

forces, backed by tanks and air bombardments, pushed the invaders back northward, crossing the thirty-eighth parallel, capturing the northern Korean city of Pyongyang, and moving toward the Chinese border.

North Korea at this point appealed to the Soviet Union to send troops, but the Soviets refused. Instead of the Soviet Union, it was China that came to North Korea's rescue. The Chinese forced the UN army back southward, nearly conquering the entire Korean peninsula. UN forces, in turn, recovered, and for nearly three years the war continued as the two sides fought each other to a standstill. The war dragged on until an armistice was signed in 1953, leaving the peninsula divided along the thirty-eighth parallel, close to the original partition line that had been established by the Soviets and Americans before the war.

American soldiers load a shell into a howitzer during the Korean War. U.S. forces joined the conflict shortly after North Korea invaded South Korea in June 1950.

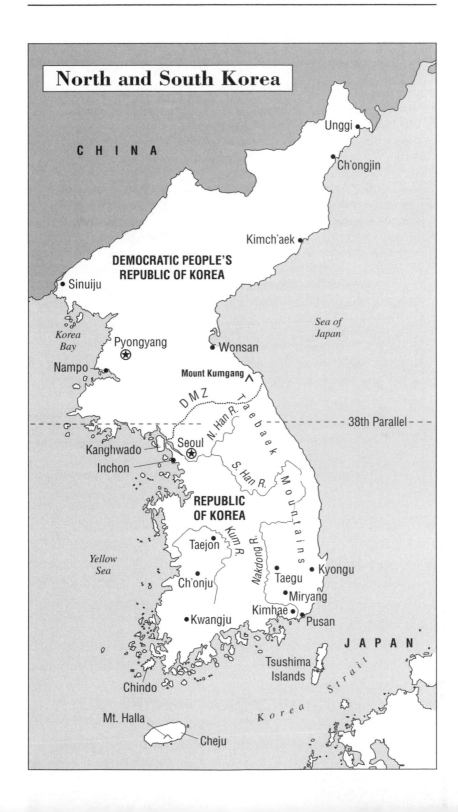

North and South Korea

CHINA

Unggi

Ch'ongjin

Kimch'aek

**DEMOCRATIC PEOPLE'S
REPUBLIC OF KOREA**

Sinuiju

*Korea
Bay*

Pyongyang

*Sea of
Japan*

Wonsan

Nampo

Mount Kumgang

DMZ

N. Han R.

Taebaek

- - - - - - - - - - 38th Parallel - - -

Kanghwado

Seoul

Inchon

S. Han R.

**REPUBLIC
OF KOREA**

M o u n t a i n s

*Yellow
Sea*

Taejon

Kum R.

Nakdong R.

Taegu

Kyongu

Ch'onju

Miryang

Kwangju

Kimhae

Pusan

JAPAN

Tsushima
Islands

Chindo

Korea *Strait*

Mt. Halla

Cheju

The Soviets' Role in the Korean War

The United States saw the North Korean/Soviet invasion of the South in 1950 as proof that the Soviet Union wanted to spread communism in Asia. Evidence has emerged since the fall of the Soviet Union showing this fear to be well founded. As historian Kathryn Weathersby explains in the Summer 1999 issue of the *Wilson Quarterly*, in an article called "The Korean War Revisited," despite the North's repeated claims that the attack was a defensive one caused by provocation from the South, "There is now no doubt that the original North Korean attack was a conventional military offensive planned and prepared by the Soviet Union."

A release of Soviet archival materials shows that the 1950 North Korean attack on the South was authorized by the Soviet Union after a year of pleas from North Korean leader Kim Il Sung. The Soviets agreed to the invasion because they believed, based on intelligence and speeches by American policy makers, that the United States would not defend South Korea or become involved militarily in Asia. Also, the Soviets sought control over South Korea to enhance their security; they were afraid that Japan might regain control over the peninsula or use it as a staging ground for invasions into Soviet territory, as had happened in the past.

After the war, both sides faced massive economic reconstruction as well as problems associated with stabilizing each side's government. North and South Korea also remained technically in a war stance, because although an armistice had been signed, no formal peace treaty could ever be agreed upon. Both sides placed heavy troop concentrations in the demilitarized zone or DMZ, the area along both sides of the border between North and South. In practical terms, this meant that Koreans, in both the North and South, feared that war might break out again at any moment.

Much has been written about the international significance of the Korean War and the ensuing Cold War standoff between the Soviet Union and the United States. For Korea, however, the war ended with no territorial gains for either side and with terrible destruction of the Korean population and land. Estimates are that about one-tenth of the entire Korean population was killed, wounded, or missing in the war, and property losses for both sides came close to $4 billion, a sizable figure in 1953 for these small countries.

Perhaps most significantly, Korea remained divided. Indeed, the war cemented the division between the two Koreas. As historian Bruce Cumings describes,

> One of the most important consequences of the war was the hardening of ideological and political lines between North and South. The antipathy that had developed between the opposing regimes was deepened into a blood feud among family members, extending from political leaders to the bulk of the ordinary people who had suffered at the hands of the other side. The thirteen-hundred-year-old unity of the Korean people was shattered.[6]

Communist North Korea 2

North Korea developed after the war in the image of the Soviet Union—with a Communist government, a centrally planned economy, and a leader who styled himself after Soviet strongman Joseph Stalin. In many ways, at least to outsiders, North Korea appeared to become a Soviet satellite state similar to those in Eastern Europe. North Korean leader Kim Il Sung, however, also sought close relations with China, remained wary of both his benefactors, and emphasized a uniquely Korean philosophy of *Juche*, or self-reliance. This combination of Stalinism, Chinese influence, and *Juche* created modern North Korea.

The "Great Leader" of North Korea

During and immediately after the Korean War, Kim Il Sung's first need was to consolidate his political power. Although he had been handpicked by the Soviets as North Korea's leader and had been appointed chairman of the Korean Workers' Party (KWP), which was the sole governing party of North Korea, Kim Il Sung's power was limited, at least at the beginning of his rule, by several factors.

One important factor was that throughout the war and at war's end, North Korea was essentially a Soviet "puppet" state over which the Soviets exercised great influence. Not only did the Soviets have great influence over Kim Il Sung himself as their handpicked leader, they also maintained numerous Soviet political advisers in North Korea. Moreover, the Soviets could count on the loyalty of Soviet-born Koreans who had come to North Korea with the Soviet Army at the end of World War II.

Another factor was that the KWP consisted at this time of several competing factions. The Soviet Koreans formed one significant power bloc within the KWP. The KWP was further divided among Koreans who had actively opposed the Japanese colonial forces. For example, Communists from South Korea who came north to become part of the new government made up one faction, while another faction consisted of Korean Communists who had returned from exile in China. Yet another group, the one to which Kim Il Sung belonged, was made up of former Korean guerrilla fighters from Manchuria who had fought the Japanese occupying forces and who had returned to Korea in 1945.

Slowly, during these early years, Kim Il Sung was able to increase his power by forming strategic alliances and blocking the political participation of his rivals. As writer Koon Woo Nam describes, "Kim showed himself a thoroughgoing Machiavellian. He displayed remarkable skill in balancing contending forces by mergers, making timely alliances with individuals or groups and changing such alliances when their usefulness was at an end."[7]

In the first decade of his rule, Kim Il Sung conducted a gradual purge to rid the KWP of potential rivals. He removed Soviet Koreans and members of other factions from positions of leadership by accusing them of crimes such as espionage or treason, then forcing their confessions or conducting show trials followed by their removal from power and imprisonment or execution. One of Kim Il Sung's victims, for example, was Korean Communist Pak Hon-yong, who had worked underground in Korea during the Japanese occupation and who had become foreign minister in North Korea's Communist government. In 1953 Kim Il Sung accused Pak and some of his followers of spying, leading to Pak's trial and eventual execution.

Three years later in 1956, in a pivotal victory, Kim Il Sung successfully suppressed an ideological assault made during a meeting of the KWP by activists from the Korean Communist movement who in the 1920s and 1930s had fled to exile in China. A member of this Chinese Yenan faction, Yun Kong-hum, denounced Kim Il Sung's policies. Kim Il Sung and his followers, however, repelled the attack, due largely to Kim Il

The Rise of Kim Il Sung

The rise of Kim Il Sung, from humble beginnings to his position as "Great Leader" of Communist North Korea, is a unique story. In reality, there is little concrete information about Kim Il Sung's family and early years. However, Kim Il Sung was born Kim Song-ju, one of three sons, on April 15, 1912, in a rural village near Pyongyang, North Korea's capital city. His father held various jobs, as a teacher, office worker, and herbal medicine practitioner, but remained poor. The family was Christian and both parents apparently were strong nationalists opposed to the Japanese occupation of Korea. In 1920 the family moved to Manchuria, where Kim Il Sung attended a Chinese school and learned to speak fluent Chinese.

Kim Il Sung first became involved in the Korean resistance movement when he was a teenager. He joined a youth group organized by the Chinese Communist Party and later joined one of the anti-Japanese guerrilla groups based in Manchuria in the 1930s. Thereafter, he rose to become a commander in the guerrilla army and led a division of a few hundred soldiers. As a guerrilla fighter Kim Il Sung carried out raids against the Japanese. For example, as Andrei Lankov, a scholar on North Korea, has documented in his book, *From Stalin to Kim Il Sung*, on June 4, 1937, "about 200 people under his command crossed the Chinese-Korean border and made a sudden attack on the small town of Poch'onbo"; there, they destroyed a Japanese police post and offices. During this period, Kim Il Sung met and married another guerrilla fighter, Kim Chong-suk.

Kim Il Sung's military successes as a guerrilla leader were reported in Korea and caused the Japanese to place him on their most-wanted list of Communist fighters. He eventually was forced to move into exile in the Soviet Union in 1940, after the Japanese began a concentrated effort to suppress the resistance movement in Manchuria and specifically targeted Kim Il Sung. In the Soviet Union, Kim Il Sung joined a Soviet military unit comprised of former Manchurian guerrillas, essentially a part of the Soviet Red Army, and settled into a domestic life with his wife. The couple had three children, one of whom, Kim Jong Il, is North Korea's current leader.

In 1945, after World War II, Kim Il Sung was sent by the Soviets to Pyongyang, the largest city in northern Korea. The Soviets at that time were looking for someone who could head the emerging Communist regime there and Kim Il Sung, as both a Soviet army officer and a hero of the anti-Japanese guerrilla movement, appeared to be a good candidate. A few days after his arrival in Pyongyang, Kim Il Sung was presented by the Soviets to North Koreans at a rally to honor the Soviet army's liberation of Korea. Shortly thereafter, he was appointed as chairman of the North Korean Bureau of the Communist Party of Korea and in 1946 was placed as head of the North Korean Provisional People's Committee, North Korea's provisional Communist government. Kim Il Sung remained the leader of North Korea from that time forward, until his death in 1994 at age eighty-two.

Sung's effective political skills. Kim Il Sung delayed the KWP discussion of his policies, used the delay to win support for his side, and organized his supporters to shut down the opposition speakers and to vote for repressive actions against the rebels. As a result, Yun and his leading associates once again fled to China; others from the Yenan faction were purged from the KWP.

Ultimately, Kim Il Sung managed to get rid of all other factions, leaving the Korean Communist guerrillas from Manchuria as the overwhelming majority in the KWP. By the early 1960s Kim Il Sung had established his complete control as dictator of North Korea.

To further enhance his power, Kim Il Sung also developed a "cult of personality" around himself similar to that created by Joseph Stalin in the Soviet Union. The Soviets themselves had begun this process when they emphasized Kim Il Sung's heroic guerrilla exploits as they promoted him to the Korean population as their leader. Kim Il Sung later intensified the effort

Kim Il Sung (right) launched a massive propaganda campaign to encourage the Korean people to revere him as a god.

through a massive propaganda campaign. As part of this campaign, Kim Il Sung's portraits were displayed throughout the country, monuments and museums were created to glorify his achievements, and he was portrayed in books, broadcasts, and government documents as a virtual deity to the Korean people.

Juche Policy and Communist Aid

Thus empowered, Kim Il Sung began implementing a policy of national self-reliance and independence called *Juche*. Korea historian Bruce Cumings describes *Juche* as the opposite of serving or relying on foreign powers—a response to Korea's experiences with invasions and colonization, embodying a high degree of nationalism and "an assumption that Korea is the center of the world."[8] As it developed, according to historian Koon Woo Nam, the *Juche* idea became "more concrete, expressing itself in the form of political independence in the Communist bloc, a self-sufficient independent economy, and self-reliance in national defense."[9]

In practical terms, *Juche* meant that North Korea, after the war, distanced itself from the Soviet Union and aligned itself more closely with the People's Republic of China, while still taking a position of relative neutrality and independence between the two countries. North Korea thus made a point of never aligning itself politically or in foreign policy with either of its benefactors. At the same time, largely by exploiting the differences between the Soviet Union and China and playing one side against the other, Kim Il Sung acquired the economic aid and protection North Korea needed to survive.

Indeed, the policy of *Juche* was possible because of tensions that had developed between China and the Soviet Union. During the years 1956 to 1957, China pulled away from the Soviet Union's influence and asserted its independence as a Communist power. This Sino-Soviet conflict thus created two separate, large Communist power centers and allowed smaller Communist states, among them North Korea, to maintain a

The Confucian Roots of the *Juche* Philosophy

Kim Il Sung, North Korea's leader until his death in 1994, encouraged a philosophy or ideology called *Juche*, which roughly translated from Korean means self-reliance or independence. As implemented by North Korea, *Juche* did result in policies of independence from the Soviet Union and China, and it also incorporated policies similar to those used by Joseph Stalin in the Soviet Union, including a cult of personality, isolationism, and militarism. Another aspect of *Juche* is its incorporation of Confucian concepts embedded in Korea as a result of centuries of Chinese influence. This Confucian view compares the political system to the human body, where the country's leader is like the brain and the people are the body that must carry out the leader's decisions and commands. A similar analogy applicable in Confucianism is that of a wise, all-knowing father/leader who takes care of a loyal family/people. North Koreans were familiar and comfortable with these concepts, and Kim Il Sung was able to use them in propaganda to encourage a type of collective political loyalty to support his totalitarian dictatorship. As North Korean analyst Bruce Cumings explains in his book *Korea's Place in the Sun*, North Korean biographers of Kim Il Sung described him in "moral language, bathing Kim in a hundred virtues, almost all of which are Confucian virtues—benevolence, love, trust, obedience, respect, reciprocity between leader and led." Kim Il Sung thus was portrayed and worshiped as a Confucian patriarch, a hero, and a genius who was guiding North Korea and who must be provided complete loyalty by his people. In this way, *Juche* helped to mobilize strong internal support for the North Korean political regime.

degree of political independence. North Korea thus was able to turn from the Soviets to the Chinese, and vice versa, for aid and support while maintaining its own foreign policy stances.

The Soviet–North Korean Tensions

Although the Soviets had provided prodigious aid and ideological support to North Korea early in its nationhood, relations between North Korea and the Chinese historically had been warmer than Soviet-Korean ties due to shared traditions and culture, and to China's help to Koreans during the Japanese occupation. Later, when the Soviet Union refused to commit its troops to support North Korea during the Korean War, forcing North Korea to turn to the Chinese for military support, the Soviets' influence began to recede in favor of the Chinese.

In addition, shortly after the war ended in 1953, the Soviet Union's new leader, Nikita Khrushchev, launched a campaign seeking to discredit many aspects of Joseph Stalin's rule. North Korea, however, like a few other Communist-bloc countries such as Romania, Albania, and China, rejected this de-Stalinization campaign. North Korea and these other countries clung to Stalinist patterns, which historian and scholar Andrei Lankov describes as including "the personality cult of a near-divine leader; militant and, occasionally, confrontational foreign policy; mass mobilization campaigns of great intensity; increasing incorporation of nationalist and chauvinist elements into the official ideology; a bias towards isolationist policies, and so on."[10] Nevertheless, playing one against the other, North Korea in 1961 convinced both the Soviets and Communist China to sign mutual defense treaties to guarantee its security against military attack by South Korea. Still, the Soviets were decreasing their assistance to North Korea.

Thereafter relations became even cooler between the Soviets and North Korea. North Korea publicly attacked the Soviets, claiming that the Soviets had no right to control North Korean Communists and aligned itself even more with China, causing the Soviets to cut off economic and military aid in 1962. North Korea, during this period, emphasized *Juche* and worked to develop its military and increase its economic output through economic programs modeled after those used by China. China did not provide enough aid to fill the void left by the Soviet withdrawal, however. As scholar Ilpyong J. Kim notes, "In the 1962–64 period the Chinese supplied $150 million in loans, while the Soviets cut off their aid to North Korea in 1962 after providing some $56 million worth of goods . . . during the 1961–62 period."[11]

Later in 1965, after the downfall of Khrushchev, the Soviets restored aid to North Korea and the two countries resumed friendly relations. The Soviets again provided North Korea with economic aid in the form of substantial loans for industrial machinery and equipment, more trade, and help in strengthening North Korea's military. Ultimately, while North Korea often leaned toward China politically, the Soviet Union became North Korea's primary economic supporter. Indeed, in its study of North Korea, the Library of Congress estimates that between 1946 and 1984 North Korea accepted "approximately $4.75 billion in economic assistance. . . . Almost 46 percent of the assistance came from the Soviet Union, followed by China with about 18 percent, and the rest from East European communist countries."[12]

At the same time his country was receiving the renewed Soviet aid, Kim Il Sung openly pursued his own course in foreign policy, stating in a December 16, 1967, speech that North Korea was now in "a position to enter the international arena on an equal footing with the people of big and small countries."[13] Thereafter, Kim Il Sung undertook a campaign of Third World diplomacy aimed at increasing North Korea's solidarity with other developing countries, expanding its base of support, and improving its international status. This policy culminated in the diplomatic recognition of North Korea by ninety-three countries by the mid-1970s and in the admission of North Korea to the World Health Organization (WHO), special agency of the United Nations (UN). WHO membership, in turn, gave North Korea observer status at the UN.

Economic Development

Kim Il Sung's biggest achievement, however, apart from consolidation of his domestic power base, was a rapid recovery from the war's economic devastation. After the war, North Korea faced enormous challenges of economic reconstruction. In the North, the war had resulted in the destruction of industry and agriculture; virtually all cities, towns, and villages had been completely destroyed. As journalist and author Geoff Simons describes,

By the end of the war much of the surviving population of North Korea was living in caves or holes in the ground. Every possible target—factories, power stations,

A napalm bomb explodes as it strikes a North Korean mining complex. Thousands of North Koreans were killed or disabled by napalm blasts during the war.

communication facilities, oil refineries, dams—had been hit. With a collapsed economy the DPRK [North Korea] was forced to cope with hundreds of thousands of orphans, the blind and the limbless, with countless thousands of victims disabled or traumatized by napalm. This is the background against which the post-war chronology of the DPRK should be considered.[14]

The North, however, blessed with a wealth of natural resources, massive Soviet aid, and a highly organized political structure, made a quick economic recovery.

Kim Il Sung achieved his economic miracle by implementing an authoritarian, state-managed, centralized economic structure in North Korea. All means of economic production were owned either by citizens organized as cooperatives or by the state. This was a command economy, responding not to market demands as does a capitalist economy, but rather to plans and goals set by the government. In addition, the North

Korean economy was based on heavy industry. As Kim Il Sung explained,

> Our Party's line in the building of heavy industry was to create our own solid bases of heavy industry which would be able to produce at home most of the raw materials, fuel, power, machines and equipment needed for the development of the national economy by relying on the rich natural resources and sources of raw materials in our country.[15]

The first priority of this government-run economy was government ownership of industry. Industry had been nationalized early on during the Soviet occupation of North Korea, and one of the first steps taken by Kim Il Sung following the war was a massive reorganization of agriculture to require farmers to work in collectives under common ownership and receive a share of profits based on their labor contribution. At the same time, Kim

Kim Il Sung encouraged laborers to work faster and more efficiently in order to help North Korea's economy. Here, the North Korean leader visits workers at a machine plant in 1967.

Il Sung launched ideologically based economic campaigns similar to Chinese programs designed to maximize labor output and increase production by urging workers to work faster and more efficiently; this system was applied first to agriculture and then to industry. After an initial period of reconstruction from 1953 to 1955, Kim Il Sung in 1956 announced a three-year plan of economic development which emphasized the control features of the command economic model and relied on significant amounts of Soviet aid.

North Korea completed the plan ahead of schedule. North Korea's initial economic achievements were hailed, even by the West, as miraculous. For example, Joan Robinson, a well-known British economist, following a visit to North Korea in 1964 described it as "a nation without poverty," and commented that "all the economic miracles of the postwar world are put in the shade"[16] compared to North Korea's achievements.

This initial economic success thus provided North Korea a certain amount of legitimacy as compared to the South Korean government, which struggled economically after the war. In the South, economic reconstruction proceeded slowly in the 1950s amid political instability and controversy surrounding what had become an autocratic and unpopular Syngman Rhee dictatorship, followed by a military government led by president Park Chung Hee. South Korea, bolstered by U.S. aid, made greater economic progress later in the 1960s, finally providing stability and improved living conditions for the populace.

Economic Slowing

Just when the South's economy began to improve in the 1960s, however, economic growth in North Korea slowed considerably. A seven-year plan of economic development was extended because of lack of progress, and subsequent plans also proved ineffective. As a result of *Juche* and some of Kim Il Sung's independent political stances, aid from the Soviets had begun to decline. Massive expenditures by the government on the military further stressed the economy. In addition, the North was burdened by a state-controlled economy that lacked the

North Korea's Human Rights Record

A human rights report published by the U.S. Department of State in 2002, entitled "Democratic People's Republic of Korea, Country Reports on Human Rights Practices—2001," summarizes the U.S. view of human rights violations in modern North Korea during 2001. It states:

> The [North Korean] Government's human rights record remained poor, and it continued to commit numerous serious abuses. Citizens do not have the right peacefully to change their government. There continued to be reports of extrajudicial killings and disappearances. Citizens are detained arbitrarily, and many are held as political prisoners; prison conditions are harsh. The constitutional provisions for an independent judiciary and fair trials are not implemented in practice. The regime subjects its citizens to rigid controls. The leadership perceives most international norms of human rights, especially individual rights, as illegitimate, alien, and subversive to the goals of the State and party. During the year, the Government entered into a human rights dialogue with the European Union, two meetings were held, but no significant results were reported. The Penal Code is Draconian, stipulating capital punishment and confiscation of assets for a wide variety of "crimes against the revolution," including defection, attempted defection, slander of the policies of the party or State, listening to foreign broadcasts, writing "reactionary" letters, and possessing reactionary printed matter. The Government prohibits freedom of speech, the press, assembly, and association, and all forms of cultural and media activities are under the tight control of the party. Radios sold in North Korea receive North Korean radio broadcasts only; radios obtained abroad by the general public must be altered to work in a similar manner. Cable News Network (CNN) television is available in one Pyongyang hotel frequented by foreigners. Under these circumstances, little outside information reaches the public except that approved and disseminated by the Government. The Government restricts freedom of religion, citizens' movements, and worker rights. There were reports of trafficking in women and young girls among refugees and workers crossing the border into China.

efficiencies demanded by market forces and suffered from typical bureaucratic inertia common among Communist economies. In the face of these pressures, North Korea's economic progress ultimately began to evaporate.

In the 1970s North Korea tried to rejuvenate its stagnant economy. A new economic program called the Three Revolutions (technological, ideological, and cultural) was launched by Kim Jong Il in the early 1970s to stimulate innovation and cut down on bureaucratic inertia. The government's efforts were made more difficult, however, by a worldwide oil shortage in 1973 that caused a sudden sharp increase in oil prices and sparked a worldwide recession. North Korea borrowed from other countries to buy Western equipment and technology to build up its industrial base, planning to repay the loans through the export of its minerals. In the recession that followed the oil crisis, however, North Korea's minerals lost much of their value, leaving the country with no way to pay its huge debt. As a result, the government defaulted to Japan, Sweden, and other countries in an amount totaling billions of dollars, making North Korea one of the world's worst credit risks. Later, in the 1980s, another policy was approved to seek joint ventures with foreign governments to improve the North Korean economy. These efforts to jump-start the North's economy, however, did not meet with great success, causing North Korea to remain dependent on assistance from the Soviet Union and China.

Isolation and Repression

Despite the deterioration of North Korea's economy, the country remained politically stable, largely due to Kim Il Sung's firm grasp on power. Like most totalitarian states, the North Korean government controlled all facets of ordinary life, including the economy, the media, and the judiciary, with no checks and balances on government activity. In addition, the KWP developed an internal police security system to ensure public obedience to state policies and suppress all dissent. Finally, North Korea succeeded in isolating its population from the outside world.

The willingness of the North Koreans to accept repression under the Communist regime is understandable in the context of history. North Korea's early economic success and the aid provided by its Communist supporters allowed it to raise the standard of living for the majority of its citizens during the 1950s and 1960s. This pleased a population used to severe poverty under the Japanese occupation and inspired early loyalty to the "Great Leader" and his policies.

Later, economic decline and the reduction of foreign aid had the opposite effect. As economic benefits decreased and food became scarce, the regime relied more and more on terror to control its starving citizens. Journalist Geoff Simons summarizes North Korea's human rights record:

Since the 1960s tens of thousands of people have been imprisoned under various forms of arbitrary detention; thousands have been tortured, with the death penalty widely used. Political prisoners have been held in camps in appalling conditions, sometimes receiving virtually no food and forced to subsist on what they could produce themselves; many have died in these detention camps.[17]

North Korea, therefore, became a country where dissent was not tolerated, run by a regime that showed a willingness to subject its people to economic deprivation, starvation, and human rights abuses in order to stay in power.

North Korea's Military and Foreign Policy

3

Kim Il Sung's postwar plan for building an independent and strong North Korea included not only efforts to develop the country's economy; it also emphasized an aggressive and self-reliant military and foreign policy. Indeed, a large part of Kim Il Sung's *Juche* philosophy focused on building up North Korea's military forces and on a foreign policy that included verbal provocations as well as the use of infiltrators, guerrilla raids, and terrorist strikes in its relations with South Korea and the United States.

Armistice Negotiations

The first sign of the North's confrontational style came shortly after the end of the Korean War. The armistice agreement that ended the fighting had left many issues, such as the question of eventual Korean reunification and ways to prevent future military confrontations, to be resolved in conferences between North and South Korea. Accordingly, a military armistice commission was created to facilitate negotiations on these issues and to monitor compliance with the armistice.

In these negotiations, however, the North used tactics such as refusing to provide advance notice of agenda items to the other side, vituperative verbal assaults during negotiations, counteraccusations, military threats, and even military raids. The North also refused to abide by terms of the armistice; it refused to let observation teams inside its borders to investigate alleged violations of the armistice and refused to permit spot checks for prohibited weapons shipments at ports of entry. Consequently, as the American Enterprise Institute's political analyst Chuck Downs has stated, "North Korea was able to bypass armistice restrictions on its military buildup and escape accountability for armistice violations."[18]

Military Buildup

To support its creation of a strong military, the North spent lavishly on its armed forces. Initially, North Korea received help from the Soviets to strengthen its military. After the decrease in assistance from the Soviets in 1962, however, the North undertook its own campaign to increase its military capabilities, spending increasing amounts of its budget on purchasing weapons and increasing the size of its armed forces. The military campaign was further heightened after a 1966 speech by Kim Il Sung that urged violent revolutionary tactics for unification. As scholar Koon Woo Nam explains, "The national economic plan for 1967 . . . was a 'tight' one . . . as a result of allocation of 30.2 percent of the total national expenditure of 1967 to military expenditure in contrast to approximately 5.6 percent annually during 1960 to 1966."[19] The military buildup escalated in the 1970s; historian Don Oberdorfer states that by 1977, when the United States completed an intensive study of intelligence data, "the North was estimated to have more men under arms than the South, whose population was twice as large."[20]

North Korea's Guerrilla War

Thwarted in his effort to reunify North and South Korea by force, Kim Il Sung turned toward a strategy of sabotage designed to start a revolution in the South that would lead to reunification of Korea under Communist leadership. Following the armistice, for example, North Korea used armistice violations, border incidents designed to raise tensions, and psychological warfare operations aimed at the South Korean armed forces to provoke the South. North Korean military agents also

North Korea's Million-Man Army

Under the leadership of Kim Il Sung and Kim Jong Il, North Korea has dedicated much of its resources toward building up its military. From its inception in 1948, North Korea has emphasized military readiness, with major campaigns to increase the size of the military in the 1960s and 1970s. According to an Associated Press article by John J. Lumpkin dated January 9, 2003, "With 1.2 million troops, the DPRK is considered the world's most militarized nation: it has more soldiers, per capita, than any other." U.S. defense officials estimate that North Korea's armed force is the fourth or fifth largest in the world, and that North Korea spends more than 30 percent of its gross domestic product on the military. In addition, more than 65 percent of North Korea's ground forces are kept within sixty miles of the demilitarized zone (DMZ), the border with South Korea, and North Korea could easily bombard Seoul, the capital of South Korea, with conventional artillery if war ever broke out again on the Korean peninsula.

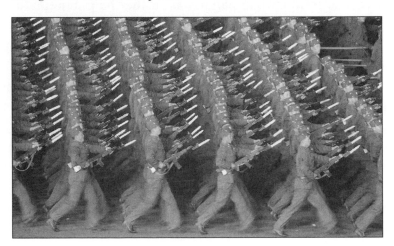

Some of North Korea's 1.2 million soldiers march during a festival in Pyongyang.

infiltrated the South in order to collect intelligence and help build a revolutionary base.

In the 1960s, however, Kim Il Sung made a clear shift toward a more violent strategy aimed at destabilizing the South Korean government, weakening U.S. support, and inspiring South Koreans to rise up to join the North and unify

Korea. Kim Il Sung openly admitted to this objective, writing, "The ultimate objective of the Party [the KWP] is to build socialist and communist society, while its immediate objective is to carry out a people's democratic revolution against U.S. imperialism and fascist rule in South Korea, overthrowing the corrupt colonial and semi-feudal social system and setting up a people's democratic regime on its grave."[21]

To accomplish this, the North adopted a strategy of guerrilla warfare, as evidenced by numerous acts of military aggression against South Korean and U.S. targets. As conservative analyst Chuck Downs notes, "From 1966 through 1969, North Korea instigated 241 armed attacks on U.S. and South Korean military personnel."[22] These attacks included attempts to assassinate South Korean presidents, attacks on ships and aircraft, and military raids. For example, between 1967 and 1969, North Korea sank a South Korean navy patrol boat, sent armed military infiltrators to attack the South Korean president, seized the U.S. Navy ship USS *Pueblo*, landed a military force of 120 in South Korea, and shot down a U.S. Navy spy plane. According to a Library of Congress history of North Korea, "The raids peaked in 1968, when more than 600 infiltrations were reported, including an unsuccessful commando attack on the South Korean presidential mansion . . . [in which] twenty-eight infiltrators and thirty-seven South Koreans were killed."[23] Also, according to the Library of Congress, "That same year [1968], 120 commandos infiltrated two east coast provinces in an unsuccessful attempt to organize a Vietnamese-type guerrilla war. In 1969 over 150 infiltrations were attempted, involving almost 400 agents."[24]

Similar incidents, some large, some small, occurred during the 1970s. In 1970, for example, a North Korean infiltrator was killed while planting a bomb intended to kill South Korean president Park Chung Hee at the Seoul National Cemetery. In 1974 North Korea again attempted an assassination of Park Chung Hee, instead killing his wife. That same year South Korea discovered that North Korea was building a labyrinth of invasion tunnels under the DMZ, which threatened the South with the possibility of a surprise attack from behind its border defense lines. Also, in a grisly incident in 1976 North Korean guards without provocation attacked a group of UN security workers who were pruning a tree at a UN checkpoint in the DMZ; the North Koreans used axes the workers had with them for tree pruning to kill two Americans and wound several others. The following year the North shot down a U.S. Army helicopter after it strayed over the DMZ killing three Americans. The North also continued its infiltration again to South Korea; as analyst Chuck Downs states, "Between July 1979 and August 1983, seven infiltrations of North Korean vessels carrying commandos and four of ground forces who had crossed through the DMZ and the Han River estuary were discovered."[25]

North Korea's infiltration efforts, however, slowed as South Korea became effective at intercepting its agents. Instead, the North emphasized assassination of South Korean leaders and

South Korean soldiers patrol one of the tunnels North Korea built under the DMZ.

terrorism against civilians. For example, in 1982, according to the testimony of a defector, the North planned but canceled a plot to assassinate South Korean president Chun Doo Hwan. In 1983 the North went forward with an attack on the South Korean president. North Korean agents detonated a bomb as South Korea's president Chun Doo Hwan met with his cabinet in Rangoon, Burma; the bomb did not harm the president, but it killed seventeen other Koreans and four Burmese. Later in the decade, in 1987, a North Korean agent bombed a South Korean Air Lines flight, killing 115 passengers and earning North Korea a place on the U.S. list of countries that practice terrorism.

Coercive Diplomacy

Although North Korea continued its strategy of military attacks and terror strikes, beginning in the early 1970s it simultaneously began to pursue negotiations with the South and the United States. The North, however, employed a provocative and confrontational style that produced few peaceful results, leading some observers to conclude that diplomacy was used simply as another means to achieve military goals of reunification on North Korea's terms.

An example of the North's negotiating style was shown in 1972 when North and South Korea began negotiations over issues of unification and other matters. A frustrated member of the South's negotiating team describes the typical course of the negotiations during the 1972 talks:

> In the first phase, the North Korean side induced its counterpart to negotiations and tried to reach "agreements in principle," the details of which could be worked out later. In the second phase, the North tried to secure advantageous detailed agreements by interpreting the above "agreements in principle" in arbitrary ways. In the last phase, in the case of disagreements, North Korea discontinued the talks unilaterally while blaming the failure of the agreements on the South Korean side.[26]

North Korea Terrorism

After the Korean War, North Korea conducted an aggressive infiltration and destabilization campaign aimed at fomenting revolution
in the South. This campaign sent military infiltrators into the South,
struck South Korean military targets, and caused skirmishes at the
DMZ. Researcher Yongho Kim claims that in addition, the North
made terrorist attacks on civilian places or targets. In an article
written for the Spring 2002 issue of the *Korean Journal of Defense
Analysis*, "North Korea's Use of Terror and Coercive Diplomacy:
Looking for Their Circumstantial Variants," Yongho Kim identified
thirty-one terrorist attacks by North Korea on civilian targets in
South Korea between 1953 and 1990:

February 16, 1958	Hijacking of a KNA airplane with 34 passengers
December 6, 1958	Kidnapping of 7 fishing boats including 42 crewmen
July 22, 1960	Firing at a vessel heading to Inchon, killing one crewman
December 15, 1960	Attempted kidnapping of the passenger vessel *Kyongju*
March 20, 1964	Kidnapping of 2 fishing boats including 26 crewmen
October 29, 1965	Kidnapping of 109 fishermen who were picking clams
November 19, 1966	Kidnapping of a fishing boat
November 3, 1967	Kidnapping of 10 fishing boats including 81 crew
December 25, 1967	Kidnapping of 4 fishing boats including 34 crew
January 6, 1968	Kidnapping of 3 fishing boats including 31 crew
January 21, 1968	Armed raid almost reaching the ROK president's office
June 17, 1968	Kidnapping of 5 fishing boats

The first phase of these negotiations resulted in a surprising
public agreement called the South-North joint communiqué, in
which the two sides agreed that unification should be peaceful
and that the two Koreas would cooperate to create an atmos-
phere of trust. Later, however, the North refused to make firm
commitments, made demands the South deemed unreasonable,
and finally abruptly ended the talks altogether when the South

October 30, 1968	Armed guerilla killing of civilians in Ulchin and Samch'ok
December 9, 1968	Killing of student Lee Seung-bok and his family
December 11, 1969	Hijacking of a South Korean airliner with 51 passengers
June 22, 1970	Assassination attempt on ROK president, National Cemetary
January 23, 1971	Attempted hijacking of a Korean Air airliner
February 4, 1972	Kidnapping of 5 fishing boats after wrecking one
August 15, 1974	Attempted assassination of ROK president (killing the first lady)
August 30, 1976	Kidnapping of the fishing boat *Shinshin III*
January 22, 1980	Kidnapping of two fishing boats
September 8, 1980	Kidnapping of the fishing boat *T'aech'ang*
1981	Assassination attempt on a visiting ROK president in Canada
October 9, 1983	Assassination attempt on ROK president in Rangoon, killing several cabinet ministers
September 24, 1984	Killing of a woman at a restaurant in Taegu
October 14, 1986	Bombing at Kimpo International Airport
November 29, 1987	Bombing of Korean Air Flight 858
January 28, 1989	Kidnapping of 2 fishing boats including 21 crew
May 4, 1989	Attempted kidnapping of 1 fishing boat
May 7, 1989	Kidnapping of 1 fishing boat including 4 crew

would not agree to its major demands. One of these demands, sought repeatedly over the years by the North, was the withdrawal of U.S. troops from South Korea, a concession the South had always ardently rejected due to North Korea's history of aggression and superior military strength.

North Korea's propensity for making demands that were sure to be rejected continued in later talks with the South.

When South Korea's President Park was assassinated by the head of the South Korean Central Intelligence Agency in 1979, the North took advantage of the instability in the South to again propose unification talks. These talks, however, also proved unsuccessful when the North employed its typical obstructions and the parties could not even agree on an agenda. Similarly, in 1981 South Korea's new president, Chun Doo Hwan, invited Kim Il Sung to visit South Korea, but the North replied by imposing preconditions the South found unacceptable, such as the creation of a new South Korean Communist government and, of course, the withdrawal of U.S. forces.

Following the failed assassination attempt on President Chun Doo Hwan in 1983, however, the North made conciliatory gestures. It agreed to hold three-way peace talks with the United States and South Korea, which the United States had earlier proposed, and it sent a goodwill gesture of food and medicine to the South following floods in 1984. Secret meetings between North and South representatives in 1985, designed to pave the way for a summit between the Korean leaders, however, once again ended when the North began arguing over details and making demands such as the cancellation of a planned joint U.S.–South Korea military exercise, Team Spirit '86. North Korea then resumed its hostile behavior toward the South, accusing the South of armistice violations and taking other actions to derail the 1988 Olympics, which were scheduled to be held in South Korea.

A Nuclear North Korea

North Korea's efforts to modernize and build its military took an ominous turn in the late 1980s and 1990s, when the North sought to add nuclear weapons and longer-range missiles to its military arsenal.

North Korea's experiments with nuclear power had begun in 1962 when it acquired a small two-megawatt nuclear reactor from the Soviet Union for research purposes. The North permitted international inspections of this facility by the UN's International Atomic Energy Agency (IAEA), aimed at ensuring that it was being used for peaceful purposes. In 1974 North Korean scientists modernized the Soviet reactor, bringing its capacity up to eight megawatts. During this period, North Korea also began to build a second research reactor.

In 1985, after much pressure and in exchange for Soviet promises to supply four light-water nuclear reactors, the North signed the Treaty on the Non-Proliferation of Nuclear Weapons (NPT) but did not agree at this time to IAEA inspections of its nuclear facilities under this agreement. Instead, North Korea completed construction of a twenty-five-megawatt, gas–graphite reactor capable of producing weapons-grade plutonium. It also began construction of a two-hundred-megawatt nuclear reactor.

Alarming Evidence

By 1989 American intelligence officials became alarmed because U.S. spy satellites detected evidence of another nuclear reactor—with a fifty-megawatt capacity—and a building that looked like a nuclear reprocessing facility—that is, a building that could house equipment to extract plutonium from nuclear-reactor fuel rods for use in nuclear weapons. This new graphite reactor, experts concluded, was capable of producing enough plutonium for ten to twelve bombs per year. The nuclear reprocessing plant could extract enough plutonium from the reactor's fuel rods to make up to forty nuclear bombs annually. Interestingly, the new facilities were built above-ground in plain view of spy satellites, suggesting the North Koreans wanted them to be seen. Historian Bruce Cumings believes that:

The DPRK probably decided in 1991, if not earlier, to develop a small-state deterrent for a country surrounded by powerful enemies, like Israel: to display enough activity to make possession of a nuclear device plausible to the outside world, but with no announcement of possession, in order to lessen the chance that those same enemies will determine to develop nuclear weapons (e.g., South Korea or Japan)—in short to appear to arm itself with an ultimate trump card and keep everyone guessing whether and when the weapons might become available.[27]

Despite its apparent intent to build nuclear weapons, and largely as a result of inducements such as the withdrawal of U.S. nuclear warheads from South Korea and the cancellation of 1992 joint U.S.–South Korea military exercises, North Korea in 1992 signed two antinuclear agreements. In one agreement, an inter-Korean Joint Declaration of the Denuclearization of the Korean Peninsula, North Korea agreed not to test, produce, or possess nuclear weapons or nuclear reprocessing facilities; the parties, however, failed to agree on an inspections program

The 1994 Framework Agreement

On October 21, 1994, following months of negotiations, the United States and North Korea signed the Agreed Framework Between the United States and the Democratic People's Republic of Korea, found in *Rogue Countries: Background and Current Issues*, edited by Alexandra Kura. The Agreed Framework ended an international crisis caused in 1993 by North Korea's admission that it was developing nuclear weapons. Under the terms of the agreement, North Korea agreed to freeze its nuclear activities in exchange for two light-water reactors designed to produce electricity and five hundred thousand metric tons of free heavy oil as an interim energy source. Specifically, the agreement provided, in part:

> Delegations of the Governments of the United States of America (U.S.) and the Democratic People's Republic of Korea (DPRK) held talks in Geneva from September 23 to October 17, 1994, to negotiate an overall resolution of the nuclear issue on the Korean peninsula. . . . The U.S. and the DPRK decided to take the following actions for the resolution of the nuclear issue:
>
> I. Both sides will cooperate to replace the DPRK's graphite-moderated reactors and related facilities with light-water reactor (LWR) power plants.
>   1) In accordance with the October 20, 1994, letter of assurance from the U.S. President, the U.S. will

to enforce this agreement. The second agreement, however, was a follow-up, implementing agreement for the nuclear nonproliferation treaty, permitting international inspections of nuclear facilities. It allowed IAEA inspections to begin in June 1992.

A Nuclear Weapons Crisis

Accordingly, the North permitted inspectors to visit its nuclear facilities in 1992, including the new reprocessing facility that had been spotted by satellites; the North Koreans even gave inspectors a sample of plutonium, admitting that a small amount had already been produced in the new reprocessing plant. Later, however, after the IAEA concluded that North

---

undertake to make arrangements for the provision to the DPRK of a LWR project with a total generating capacity of approximately 2,000 MW (e) by a target date of 2003. . . .

2) In accordance with the October 20, 1994, letter of assurance from the U.S. President, the U.S., representing the consortium, will make arrangements to offset the energy foregone due to the freeze of the DPRK's graphite-moderated reactors and related facilities, pending completion of the first LWR unit. . . .

3) Upon receipt of U.S. assurances for the provision of LWR's and for arrangement for interim energy alternatives, the DPRK will freeze its graphite-moderated reactors and related facilities and will eventually dismantle these reactors and related facilities. . . .

4) As soon as possible after the date of this document, U.S. and DPRK experts will hold two sets of expert talks. . . .

II. The two sides will move toward full normalization of political and economic relations. . . .

III. Both sides will work together for peace and security on a nuclear-free Korean peninsula. . . .

IV. Both sides will work together to strengthen the international nuclear nonproliferation regime.

Korea had produced more plutonium than it had admitted, the North refused to permit further inspections, broke off talks with the South, and threatened war if inspections or sanctions were forced upon it. In March 1993 the North increased tensions even more by threatening to withdraw from the NPT, essentially the pillar of U.S. and the international community's efforts to control nuclear proliferation around the world.

These actions by North Korea sparked an international crisis. In April 1993 the North proposed bilateral negotiations with the United States to end the crisis. After the United States agreed to talk, the North quickly suspended its withdrawal from the NPT, and these talks resulted eventually in an agreement. Despite the intervening death of North Korea's "Great Leader" Kim Il Sung in 1994 and much intransigence by the North Koreans during the negotiations (leading a frustrated United States under the Clinton administration to threaten sanctions and prepare for a military attack on the North), a framework agreement was signed in 1994 between the United States and North Korea. In the Agreed Framework, the North agreed to freeze its nuclear weapons development program, including closing its existing twenty-five-megawatt reactor and the nuclear fuel reprocessing facility as well as stopping work on two other reactors then under construction—fifty-megawatt and two-hundred-megawatt graphite reactors—in exchange for aid in the form of heavy fuel oil and light-water reactors for producing electricity. These concessions were acceptable to the United States because it is much harder to extract weapons-grade material from light-water reactors. Also, the United States promised in the agreement to work toward normalization of relations with North Korea, another goal that had by then become important to the North Koreans.

The United States, for its part, believed that by offering aid linked to cooperation it had created a means to moderate North Korean nuclear behavior in the future. It was reassured that implementation of the agreement would be placed in international hands through the creation of the Korean Peninsula

Energy Development Organization (KEDO). To many observers, however, North Korea achieved significant benefits from a crisis that it generated. As the American Enterprise Institute's Chuck Downs puts it, "By using high pressure tactics but restricting demands to concessions the rest of the world can afford to make, when the alternative appeared to be war, Kim Il Sung guaranteed his success."[28] In addition, some American nuclear experts pointed out that by agreeing only to freeze operations, North Korea managed to avoid destroying all its existing nuclear facilities as well as the two nuclear bombs that it had likely already created. Indeed, as noted by Victor Gilinsky, an appointee to the U.S. Nuclear Regulatory Commission under presidents Gerald Ford and Jimmy Carter, the agreement allowed the nuclear facilities to be reactivated at any time and thus "left the United States subject to continued blackmail."[29] These critics suggested that North Korea had no intention of completely giving up its nuclear weapons programs.

North Korea's Missile Development

In addition to developing nuclear technology which could produce nuclear weapons, in the late 1980s North Korea began to develop missiles capable of delivering the weapons to their targets. In 1993 North Korea tested a short-range ballistic missile, the two-stage Nodong (capable of striking South Korea), but the world did not take notice. Then in August 1998, North Korea launched a longer-range multistage Taepodong I missile across Japan and into the Pacific Ocean. The launch was lauded in North Korea as an example of the country's strength and military potential. Elsewhere in the world the missile firing was seen as a threatening act, proving that North Korea had developed the means of delivering warheads, whether conventional, chemical, biological, or nuclear, to South Korea and Japan. The test also demonstrated the North's growing technical capabilities and indicated that, given sufficient time, it would be able to develop intercontinental missiles capable of reaching the United States.

North Korea launches a Taepodong I missile in August 1998.

In response to the successful test, the United States sent negotiators to North Korea in an effort to convince the North to stop its missile development. Those negotiations, however, did not result in such an agreement; what was achieved instead was a unilateral North Korean moratorium on further missile tests in exchange for the lifting of U.S. economic sanctions that prohibited most U.S. exports to and imports from North Korea. The absence of an agreement banning missile development meant that North Korea could continue to develop short, medium, and possibly long-range missiles.

As a result of its decades-long emphasis on maintaining a strong military, including efforts in the 1980s and 1990s to acquire and develop nuclear and missile capabilities, North Korea continued to be seen as a formidable force in Asia and a threat to South Korea, despite internal economic problems.

The 1990s: A Time of Challenges 4

As the 1990s opened, North Korea faced a harsh new reality—the collapse of communism in the Soviet Union, North Korea's main benefactor. North Korea's alignment with communism, once a source of economic and military support, no longer brought security after the Soviets cut off aid to the North. This loss of economic support, followed by a food famine and the death of "Great Leader" Kim Il Sung, created great pressure and uncertainty for the country, forcing it to struggle for survival. Rather than abandon its Cold War legacy of communism, however, North Korea continued its tough talk and confrontational foreign policies.

The Collapse of Communism

Trouble arose for North Korea in the late 1980s when the political unity of the Soviet bloc and even the Soviet Union itself began to disintegrate. The disintegration started in 1985 when Mikhail Gorbachev became premier of the Soviet Union and began to relax restrictions on political dissent and economic activity with the reform policies of glasnost (openness) and perestroika (restructuring). Dissatisfaction with economic conditions had been on the rise throughout the Soviet bloc. Then, very quickly, demands for democratic reforms and the abandonment of Communist economic principles spread through the Communist countries, including Poland, East Germany, Czechoslovakia, Bulgaria, Romania, and Hungary. The upheaval spread to the Soviet Union itself, and in 1991 the Soviet Union completely dissolved.

Although North Korea's regime managed to avoid implementing the reforms that had led to the demise of other Communist governments, the Soviet collapse deeply affected North Korea by ending the economic subsidies on which North Korea had long relied. At the same time, economic difficulties among the former Soviet republics left these nations, which had been a market for North Korean exports, strapped for cash and unable to purchase those goods. Deprived of its traditional socialist markets, North Korea was unable to earn foreign currency. Finally, North Korea now had to pay world prices for essential goods such as oil, industrial equipment, and raw materials, which it previously had gotten at deep discounts. Indeed, both China and the Soviet Union notified North Korea in the early 1990s that it was required to use hard currency, instead of trade credits, to make purchases of necessary products. As a result of these developments, trade plummeted. For example, demographers Daniel Goodkind and Loraine West estimate that "By 1993 Russia's exports to North

A statue of Lenin is lowered in Bucharest. The fall of communism created economic uncertainty for North Korea.

Korea were only 10 percent of what had been received from the Soviet Union prior to 1991."[30]

In December 1993, in a surprising admission in an official communiqué, North Korea publicly acknowledged the tremendous blow to its economy caused by the breakup of the Soviet Union, stating that the economy was in a "grave situation" and suffering "grim trials."[31] Thereafter, North Korea hoped China could help replace the lost Soviet aid. The North also began to export arms and missiles to countries such as Iraq, Iran, and Syria to earn much-needed cash. These efforts, however, could not begin to fill the void left by the Soviet collapse.

Indeed, China had for some time been undergoing its own economic restructuring and had already been providing less and less support for North Korea. Under the leadership of Teng Hsiao-p'ing, China reformed the four sectors of its economy—agriculture, industry, the military, and science/technology—and opened China to trade with the West. China also embraced free-market reforms, allowed joint ventures with capitalists, and encouraged foreign investment. These reforms weakened China's traditional ties with North Korea; as China integrated into the world economy and increased its economic ties with the West, its trade with North Korea dropped dramatically.

Making matters even worse for North Korea was its eroding diplomatic position. As South Korea's economy steadily improved, both the Soviet Union and China began to desire closer trading relations with that nation. The Soviet Union formally recognized South Korea in January 1991, a process repeated by China in 1992. Former Soviet-bloc countries, such as Hungary, Yugoslavia, and Poland, followed suit. As South Korea pulled ahead of the North both economically and diplomatically, North Korea was left even more isolated. More economic woes lay ahead, however.

Economic Collapse in North Korea

The decrease in economic aid from Russia and China was followed by natural disasters in North Korea that threw the country into economic chaos. Floods followed by drought destroyed harvests and devastated the nation's agricultural base. By the end of the twentieth century, North Korea's population was starving and its economy was in shambles.

Even as early as 1992 there had been clear signs that North Korea was running short of food. In 1992, for example, the regime began a propaganda campaign urging North Koreans to eat only two meals a day in order to save scarce food resources. The North also quietly contacted South Korea and the United States, describing its food shortages in dire terms and asking for secret food assistance.

North Korea's situation worsened in 1995 and 1996, when the country experienced a series of devastating floods. The 1995 rains were severe enough to destroy crops, but as writer Han S. Park states, "Heavy rainfall and floods swept away as much as 40 percent of the arable land in 1996,"[32] causing long-term destruction of agricultural production. The rains further disabled North Korea's agrarian economy and resulted in homelessness, famine, and mass starvation.

These emaciated North Korean boys suffer from malnutrition as a result of the country's crop failures in the mid-1990s.

The rains were followed in 1997 by a serious drought and tidal waves along North Korea's western coast. These disasters damaged farmland even more and added to North Korea's food shortage. The North Korean government keeps secret just how many people died from the famine, but demographers Daniel Goodkind and Loraine West note that as of 2001 estimates ran as high as 2 million deaths from starvation and related causes since the start of the crisis: If true, this figure "would constitute almost 10 percent of North Korea's 1993 population of 21 million"[33]—a huge loss for the small country.

In the years following these natural disasters, North Korea's entire economy seemed to implode. Factories closed due to the lack of fuel oil necessary for operation, and modern forms of transportation such as trains were idled. Electrical blackouts became common. Even the state-run television station was occasionally forced off the air due to lack of power to run its transmitters. Food production, already battered by flooding and erosion, declined further as the factories that produced necessary fertilizer closed. Even the food that was produced could not be properly distributed due to lack of fuel for trucks and trains to carry the harvested crops. Starving North Koreans were reduced to eating grass and tree bark, bartering goods at black markets for food, and scavenging factories for scrap metal to be sold across the border to the Chinese. Analysts believe that the regime even had difficulty feeding its army, as evidenced by a speech by Kim Jong Il in 1997, in which he urged the public to send rice to soldiers.

One measure of the depth of the famine was the growing number of North Koreans who risked terrible reprisals by the North's regime to flee across the border to China. China considered these people to be economic migrants, rather than political refugees. Nevertheless, China allowed many of the refugees to leave for destinations like the Philippines, from which many then departed for South Korea. Tens, perhaps hundreds, of thousands of refugees chose this escape in the 1990s.

The seriousness of North Korea's economic situation, however, was perhaps best illustrated by its willingness to

Famine and Food Rationing in North Korea

North Koreans have suffered from a lack of food since the early 1990s, when the cutoff of Soviet aid and natural disasters caused a severe food famine and left the country unable to recover without massive food aid from the United Nations and other countries. Some North Koreans had fled to China to escape starvation.

The government provides food rations but, according to the testimony of women refugees in China provided to Amnesty International, the rations are unequally distributed depending on social status, occupation, and age. For example, as quoted by Nicolette Jackson and Sean Healy in an article in the September 2002 issue of the *New Internationalist*, "Desperate Escape: The Backbreaking Work of North Korean Women," refugees state:

> The first class comprises senior party members and close associates of (the country's President) Kim Jung Il who are entitled to a daily ration of meat, cooking oil, fruit, vegetables and cigarettes. The second class of people (including central party members, government officials and high-ranking military officers) is entitled to a weekly ration. The third class of people (such as junior members of the party and families of anti-Japanese guerrilla fighters) is entitled to a ration every other week.

Apparently, ordinary people receive only one ration of rice every two weeks. For most people, these rations provide no more than half the recommended amount of nutrition. As a result, those who can afford it buy supplemental food at farmers markets, where prices are high due to great demand. There are reports that people in North Korea are quitting school and jobs to scrounge for food, and that they are eating grass and seaweed to survive.

Although not as severe as during the 1990s, the famine continued in 2002 and 2003, when the United Nation's World Food Program (WFP), the primary provider of food to the country, experienced a drop in contributions from donating countries. Japan and the United States completely cut off their contributions to the WFP in 2002 because of North Korea's nuclear weapons issues and tough political stance. On February 25, 2003, the United States announced that it would resume shipments of food aid to North Korea, but said it would cut donations in 2003 between 35 and 75 percent from last year's totals. China also provides food assistance to North Korea in a bilateral donation separate from the WFP program.

A Japanese government employee takes stock of pallets of rice that will be donated to North Korea as part of a relief effort.

abandon its *Juche* ideals to survive. As historian Don Oberdorfer notes, in 1995, "for the first time in its history, the bastion of self-reliance openly appealed to the world for help, asking the United Nations [UN] for nearly $500 million in flood relief as well as fuel and medical assistance."[34] The UN agreed to help but demanded access to flood-ravaged areas to assure that aid would reach Koreans most affected. When the UN observers visited North Korea in late 1995, Oberdorfer relates, they found "people scavenging in the fields looking for roots and wild plants to prepare soup for their families."[35] As a result, South Korea, Japan, and the United States responded to UN food appeals and provided food aid to the North Koreans.

No one really knows, however, how much of the food aid provided to North Korea actually reached its population; according to researchers Daniel Goodkind and Loraine West, "of all food aid received by North Korea only 10 percent goes directly to hungry civilians, while 10 percent is diverted to the military and 80 percent ends up in the hands of government officials."[36]

The New "Dear Leader"

North Korea's situation was made all the more difficult by political uncertainty when its leader, Kim Il Sung, died of a heart attack on July 8, 1994, at age eighty-two. Although his death at that particular time was unexpected, Kim Il Sung had prepared for the event by naming his son, Kim Jong Il, as his successor. Many observers had predicted that the Communist regime in North Korea would not survive Kim Il Sung's passing. They were proven wrong, however, as Kim Jong Il seized the reigns after his father's death and continued all facets of his father's regime.

Little was known about Kim Jong Il before he became North Korea's new leader. Although Kim had worked for the KWP for many years, he had not been visible to the outside world until October 1980, when he was given various new posts in the North Korean government, designated as Kim Il Sung's successor, and awarded the title of "Dear Leader." Thereafter, the North Korean government heavily promoted the younger Kim, placing his portraits everywhere alongside his father's and glorifying his achievements and intelligence.

What was known about the younger leader before he succeeded his father was that he had been linked with terrorist acts against South Korea and its citizens, suggesting that North Korea would be likely to continue its hostile relationship with South Korea. In 1978, for example, Kim Jong Il reportedly arranged for a prominent South Korean actress, Choi Eun Hee, to be kidnapped along with her husband and held in North Korea for three years to work with Kim Jong Il to develop North Korea's film industry. The younger Kim also was believed to be responsible for the 1983 bombing of South Korean cabinet members at Rangoon and the 1987 bombing of Korean Air Lines Flight 858 that killed 115 people.

Indeed, after he succeeded his father in 1994 Kim Jong Il quickly signaled that he would continue the militancy and hard bargaining for which his father had been famous. He completed negotiations that his father had begun with the United

States on North Korea's nuclear weapons development, acquiring the concessions of fuel oil and light-water reactors to produce electricity. Soon thereafter, in December 1994, North Korea shot down a U.S. Army helicopter that had strayed into North Korean airspace and refused to release the surviving copilot.

Kim Jong Il:
North Korea's "Dear Leader"

Kim Jong Il, North Korea's current leader, was born on February 16, 1942, in the Soviet Union while his father, Kim Il Sung, was in exile there following his anti-Japanese guerrilla activity during the Japanese occupation of Korea. After the Japanese surrender at the end of World War II in 1945, Kim Jong Il returned to Korea with his family when his father was selected by the Soviet Union to head the new North Korean government, but he was evacuated to China during the Korean War. Kim Jong Il was one of three children, two boys and a girl, but his younger brother accidentally drowned and his mother died giving birth to a stillborn baby while Kim Jong Il was young. His father remarried in the early 1960s and produced four half-siblings for Kim Jong Il, two boys and two girls.

In 1964 Kim Jong Il graduated from Kim Il Sung University with a political-economy degree and thereafter worked for the Central Committee of the Korean Workers' Party (KWP) for several years, responsible for films, theater, and art—his major areas of interest. In 1973 he became a secretary of the Central Committee, and a member of its politburo the following year. In October 1980 he was appointed to senior posts in the North Korean government and was proclaimed as Kim Il Sung's designated successor. North Korea's government also gave him the title of "Dear Leader," close to his father's title of "Great Leader." When his father died in 1994 Kim Il Sung took over as leader of North Korea and has remained in power ever since.

Before he came to power Kim Jong Il was viewed by the outside world mostly as a playboy who wore stylish clothes, loved to party, and preferred the company of beautiful women. Since then his reputation has grown, because he has shown intelligence and a keen understanding of issues when meeting with outside officials and heads of state such as South Korean president Kim Dae Jung and U.S. secretary of state Madeleine Albright. Defectors describe Kim Jong Il as paranoid and harsh with opponents, and completely serious about his duties as leader of North Korea.

Foreign Engagement and Economic Concessions

Even before the death of Kim Il Sung, economic problems appeared to place new pressure on North Korea to negotiate with its traditional enemies—the United States and South Korea—in order to acquire food and other economic aid necessary for its survival. North Korea, however, approached and conducted these negotiations in its typical provocative style.

The first indications of conciliatory behavior from North Korea in the early 1990s, for example, included a 1991 abandonment of its historic claim to be the only legitimate Korean government, and its agreement to participate as a member of the United Nations simultaneously with South Korea. Also, it was in the early 1990s that North Korea signed agreements relating to denuclearization.

By the late 1990s acquiring food became the critical foreign-policy focus for North Korea. The North openly negotiated for assistance, linking its participation in peace talks with the United States and South Korea for reduction of military tensions on the Korean peninsula to the provision of humanitarian aid. For example, during discussions with the United States in 1996, according to Don Oberdorfer, the North bluntly told U.S. negotiators "the North could either sell missiles to Middle Eastern countries to obtain money and food, as it had formerly done to American disapproval, or it could accept food from the United States to forego those sales."[37] Similarly, North Korea in 1997 agreed to the four-way peace talks that it previously had rejected, first demanding food aid as a precondition of its participation. Also, when U.S. intelligence in 1998 detected what appeared to be a secret underground nuclear weapons facility, North Korea permitted inspections of the site, again in exchange for aid.

Negotiating with the South

Experts believe that North Korea's economic straits also may have caused it to negotiate with South Korea, which at the same time was displaying a new interest in reconciling with its neighbor. In 1998 Kim Dae Jung was elected as president of South Korea and implemented a new policy of engagement toward the North called his "Sunshine Policy," founded on three principles that he enunciated in his inaugural address: "First, [South Korea] will never tolerate armed provocation of any kind. Second, we do not have any intention to undermine or absorb North Korea. Third, we will actively push reconciliation and cooperation between the South and North beginning with those areas which can be most easily agreed upon."[38]

Kim Dae Jung's program began amid typical North Korean military threats, including both the 1998 missile test over Japan and a June 1999 naval clash, the first serious naval clash with South Korea since the Korean War. North Korean crab-fishing boats accompanied by North Korean military patrol vessels crossed into South Korean waters, where they were confronted by South Korean patrols. The North Korean boats began firing on the South Korean vessels, leading to a gun battle in which the South sank a North Korean torpedo boat and its crew.

In June 2000, however, Kim Jong Il agreed to meet directly with Kim Dae Jung. In what was viewed as a historic summit, the two leaders agreed to a joint declaration stating the desire of the two Koreas to resolve the question of unification by themselves and agreeing to promote trust through various programs such as family reunions and civic, cultural,

Kim Jong Il (pictured) speaks at a historic meeting with Kim Dae Jung in June 2000.

Summit Agreement Between North and South Korea

In June 2000 North Korean leader Kim Jong Il and South Korean president Kim Dae Jung met in North Korea in a historic summit meeting. During the meeting, the two leaders agreed to a joint declaration, which as quoted on a website run by Radio Veritas Asia, an Asian missionary group, provided:

> True to the noble will of all the fellow countrymen for the peaceful reunification of the country, Chairman Kim Jong-Il of the National Defense Commission of the Democratic People's Republic of Korea and President Kim Dae-Jung of the Republic of Korea had a historic meeting and summit in Pyongyang from June 13 to 15, 2000. The heads of the North and the South, considering that the recent meeting and summit, the first of their kind in history of division, are events of weighty importance in promoting mutual understanding, developing inter-Korean relations and achieving peaceful reunification, declare as follows:
>
> 1. The North and the South agreed to solve the question of the country's reunification independently by the concerted efforts of the Korean nation responsible for it.
>
> 2. The North and the South, recognizing that a proposal for federation of lower stage advanced by the North side and a proposal for confederation put forth by the South side for the reunification of the country have elements in common, agreed to work for the reunification in this direction in the future.
>
> 3. The North and the South agreed to settle humanitarian issues, including exchange of visiting groups of separated families and relatives and the issue of unconverted long-term prisoners, as early as possible on the occasion of August 15 this year.
>
> 4. The North and the South agreed to promote the balanced development of the national economy through economic cooperation and build mutual confidence by activating cooperation and exchanges in all fields, social, cultural, sports, public health, environmental and so on.
>
> 5. The North and the South agreed to hold dialogues between the authorities as soon as possible to implement the above-mentioned agreed points in the near future.
>
> 6. President Kim Dae-Jung cordially invited Chairman Kim Jong-Il of the DPRK National Defense Commission to visit Seoul and Chairman Kim Jong-Il agreed to visit Seoul at an appropriate time in the future.

A North Korean man cries as he is reunited with his sisters in Seoul. The June 2000 summit meeting between Kim Jong Il and Kim Dae Jung made such family reunions possible.

sports, public health, and environmental exchanges. The leaders also announced that Kim Jong Il would visit South Korea in the future.

In the first year after the summit the two Koreas held additional talks and made progress on several cooperative actions, including reunions for family members, economic ventures, and social/cultural/sports exchanges. For example, by August 2001, three rounds of reunions of separated family members had been arranged, and a total of thirty-six hundred persons met with their relatives from whom they had been separated since the war. In addition, several economic ventures were started, including a reconnection of a railway line between Seoul, South Korea, and Sinuiju, North Korea. Other proposed projects included an industrial complex in the Gaeseong area of North Korea, built by the Hyundai Group, and a joint flood prevention project for the Imjin River, which runs on the border between the two countries. Also, some tourism projects met with some success, as well as several social/cultural/sports exchanges between North and South—of individuals, executives, media professionals, symphony orchestras, opera groups, singers, and tennis players. Other cooperative efforts included South Korea's support for North Korea's membership in international organizations such as the ASEAN Regional Forum, the Asian Development Bank, and the Asia-Pacific Economic Cooperation Forum, a joint effort to achieve a UN resolution supporting the 2000 summit and unification goals, and a joint protest before the UN Commission on Human Rights over the treatment of the so-called comfort women by the Japanese during World War II.

The peace process between the two Koreas, however, was largely discontinued after March 2001, when official talks stalled. In addition, four-party international talks including North and South Korea, China, and the United States faltered and became deadlocked in August 1999, due to North Korea's refusal to participate after rejection of its repeated demands for U.S. troop withdrawal and a bilateral U.S.–North Korea peace treaty. Notably, South Korean newspapers eventually revealed that South Korean president Kim Dae Jung paid the North $200 million to make the 2000 summit meeting between the two Koreas possible, suggesting that even the peace summit was a trade for economic aid.

As the twentieth century came to a close, North Korea remained politically isolated and in economic decline, searching for economic aid, and struggling to survive.

North Korea and Weapons of Mass Destruction 5

In October 2002 North Korea once again was thrust into the forefront of world politics. A new international crisis emerged when North Korea confirmed that it had secretly resumed its efforts to develop nuclear weapons, prompted, some believe, by a more confrontational U.S. approach to North Korea.

U.S. Policy Shift

The U.S. policy toward North Korea since the early 1990s had been one of engagement, based on the idea that by negotiating with the North and providing it with food and economic aid, the United States could contain the North Korean regime's ambitions to develop nuclear weapons and missiles, both of which the United States believed would be destabilizing for the region and the world. However, the election of U.S. president George W. Bush and his inauguration in January 2001 marked a shift in U.S. policy away from that engagement. President Bush and his advisers began to consider countering North Korea's military threats with more punitive tactics, such as withdrawal of economic and food aid, use of sanctions, and possibly even military action.

The first official signal of this shift came in March 2001, when President Bush made remarks critical of South Korea's "Sunshine Policy" toward the North and announced he would undertake a review of U.S. policy regarding North Korea. That policy review, completed in June 2001, recommended continued engagement, but the Bush administration also linked progress in talks on nuclear weapons and missiles to a broader agenda, including reduction of conventional forces on the Korean peninsula and improving North Korea's human rights record.

An "Axis of Evil"

Relations with the United States took a decided turn for the worse when, following the September 11, 2001, terrorist attack on the United States, Bush began focusing America's foreign policy on a global effort to root out terrorism. In his January 2002 State of the Union address, Bush announced that the United States would stop regimes that sponsor terror from threatening the world with weapons of mass destruction, naming North Korea as one of these terrorist regimes. Bush stated:

Our . . . goal is to prevent regimes that sponsor terror from threatening America or our friends and allies with weapons of mass destruction. Some of these regimes have been pretty quiet since September the 11th. But we know their true nature. North Korea is a regime arming with missiles and weapons of mass destruction, while starving its citizens. Iran aggressively pursues these weapons and exports terror, while an unelected few repress the Iranian people's hope for

President Bush identifies North Korea as a terrorist regime during his State of the Union address.

freedom. Iraq continues to flaunt its hostility toward America and to support terror. . . . States like these, and their terrorist allies, constitute an axis of evil, arming to threaten the peace of the world. By seeking weapons of mass destruction, these regimes pose a grave and growing danger. They could provide these arms to terrorists, giving them the means to match their hatred. They could attack our allies or attempt to blackmail the United States.[39]

Bush went on to promise action against the countries he had named, saying:

In any of these cases, the price of indifference would be catastrophic. We will work closely with our coalition to deny terrorists and their state sponsors the materials, technology, and expertise to make and deliver weapons of mass destruction. We will develop and deploy effective missile defenses to protect America and our allies from sudden attack. And all nations should know: America will do what is necessary to ensure our nation's security.[40]

North Korea protested Bush's remarks, pointing out that it was the United States, not North Korea, that was making the threats. The president's words struck at the core of the regime's fears; to North Korea, they meant that the United States might be considering a military strike aimed at dislodging the Kim Jong Il regime.

In the months following the speech, the Bush administration continued its hostile rhetoric and actions toward the North. For example, President Bush made remarks such as "I loathe Kim Jong Il"[41] in an interview with the *Washington Post*'s Bob Woodward. In February, in a press conference with South Korean president Kim Dae Jung in Seoul, Bush clarified his position, but still indicated hostility toward Kim Il Jong and his government, saying that his comments were aimed at the government, not the people of North Korea. Bush went on to say that what the United States wanted was for North

Koreans to have food and freedom and committed the United States to attain those goals peacefully.

A Potential Target

North Korea was not mollified by the president's explanation. The North Korean Foreign Ministry responded, stating that "Bush made clearer the U.S. intention to violate the sovereignty of [North Korea], openly interfere in its internal affairs and stifle it by force."[42] Nor were North Korea's fears about American intentions eased when, in March 2002, a U.S. defense report called the Nuclear Posture Review identified North Korea as a potential target for American nuclear weapons. This disclosure led North Korea to warn that an attack on it would create a "global nuclear arms race" and result in "nuclear disaster."[43]

Relations deteriorated further when the United States abandoned its plans to send a high-level delegation to talk with North Korea in June 2002, after a June 29 naval battle between North and South Korea that killed at least four South Korean sailors and wounded nineteen. On August 23 the U.S. Department of State announced that it had imposed sanctions on the North Korean government for selling missile technology to Yemen. Also in August, John R. Bolton, the undersecretary of state for arms control and international security, gave a speech in Seoul, South Korea, criticizing North Korea as an "evil regime that is armed to the teeth, including with weapons of mass destruction and ballistic missiles."[44]

For its part, North Korea complained that the United States had violated the Agreed Framework and failed to implement U.S. commitments under the agreement. North Korea pointed out that the light-water reactor construction, promised by the 1994 agreement, was behind schedule and that the United States had failed to normalize relations with the North, as required by the agreement. The United States contended that the North's own actions caused the delays in construction, and that North Korea had refused to abide by the agreement's provision on nuclear weapons inspections. The agreement

U.S. President George Bush's Preemption Policy

On September 20, 2002, U.S. president George W. Bush released a report outlining a new national security policy that suggests the United States will take preemptive action against terrorists and countries that possess or are developing weapons of mass destruction. The new policy of preemption is a shift from past U.S. policy, which emphasized a defensive international posture. The report, entitled "The National Security Strategy of the United States," explains the reasons behind the policy of preemptive attack:

> The nature of the Cold War threat required the United States—with our allies and friends—to emphasize deterrence of the enemy's use of force, producing a grim strategy of mutual assured destruction. With the collapse of the Soviet Union and the end of the Cold War, our security environment has undergone profound transformation. . . .

> New deadly challenges have emerged from rogue states and terrorists. None of these contemporary threats rival the sheer destructive power that was arrayed against us by the Soviet Union. However, the nature and motivations of these new adversaries, their determination to obtain destructive powers hitherto available only to the world's strongest states, and the greater likelihood that they will use weapons of mass destruction against us, make today's security environment more complex and dangerous.

> In the 1990s we witnessed the emergence of a small number of rogue states. . . . In the past decade North Korea has become the world's principal purveyor of ballistic missiles, and has tested increasingly capable missiles while developing its own WMD arsenal. Other rogue regimes seek nuclear, biological, and chemical weapons as well. These states' pursuit of, and global trade in, such weapons has become a looming threat to all nations.

> We must be prepared to stop rogue states and their terrorist clients before they are able to threaten or use weapons of mass destruction against the United States and our allies and friends. . . .

> Given the goals of rogue states and terrorists, the United States can no longer solely rely on a reactive posture as we have in the past. The inability to deter a potential attacker, the immediacy of today's threats, and the magnitude of potential harm that could be caused by our adversaries' choice of weapons, do not permit that option. We cannot let our enemies strike first.

required North Korea to allow IAEA inspections following completion of a significant portion of the light-water reactors but before nuclear components were to be delivered; the Bush administration insisted that the North had to agree to inspections soon because the construction would be finished in two to four years, and the inspections would take that long to complete. As a result of the North's failure to submit to inspections, the Bush administration in early 2002 refused to certify that the North was in compliance with the agreement.

The New Nuclear Threat

After almost a year of heightened rhetoric and hostilities, North Korea and the United States finally agreed to talks, which were scheduled for October 2002. These talks, however, instead of resolving bilateral hostilities, precipitated yet another international crisis over North Korea's nuclear weapons. On October 19, 2002, the United States announced to the world that North Korea had admitted to possessing a nuclear weapons development program. North Korean first vice foreign minister Kang Suk Ju made the admission on October 4, 2002, during a meeting with a U.S. delegation after Assistant Secretary of State James Kelly confronted him with U.S. suspicions of the program's existence. Instead of denying it was developing nuclear weapons, North Korea not only owned up to the fact, but also stated that it had other weapons it described as "more powerful."[45] U.S. officials interpreted this to mean other types of weapons of mass destruction, such as chemical and biological weapons.

The North justified its decision to develop nuclear weapons by claiming it needed them to defend itself against the United States. For example, the North's state-run radio broadcast a statement that the North "has come to have nuclear and other strong military weapons due to nuclear threats by U.S. imperialists."[46] Later, North Korea downplayed this statement, maintaining it did not say it actually possessed nuclear weapons, only that it was "entitled" to have nuclear and other weapons. North Korea proposed a nonaggression treaty with the United States as the solution to the crisis.

The United States said that North Korea's actions placed it in violation of several antinuclear agreements, including the Agreed Framework that had been negotiated in 1994 after the previous crisis over the North's efforts to develop nuclear weapons. Notably, the new program was a uranium-enrichment program, not the plutonium-based nuclear weapons program the North promised to halt in the 1994 agreement; thus, technically, North Korea could claim it was not violating the agreement. Still, the agreement had also broadly committed North Korea to work toward a nuclear-free Korean peninsula and against nuclear proliferation.

The United States initially responded to North Korea's revelations in a hard-line manner, calling the North Korean action blackmail and refusing to negotiate until North Korea dismantled the nuclear program. On November 13, 2002, the United States also engineered the cut off of vital fuel oil promised to the North under the agreement, despite the fact that the timing of the cutoff meant that fuel oil would not be available during the bitterly cold North Korean winter. Later, U.S. officials threatened to take the matter to the UN, which could order sanctions, and made it known that it was considering a naval blockade to stop North Korean missile exports.

North Korea countered these U.S. responses by escalating the crisis. In December the North dismantled IAEA surveillance cameras which had been installed to monitor the 1994 agreement, moved spent fuel rods to a storage site near its graphite reactor in Yongbyon, threatened to reopen its plutonium-reprocessing plant, and ordered IAEA inspectors to leave the country. On January 10, 2003, North Korea said it was pulling out of the nuclear nonproliferation treaty, heightening tensions even more. North Korea also hinted that it might drop its moratorium on missile tests.

A Conciliatory Tone

In January 2003 the United States began taking a more conciliatory tone, stating its peaceful intentions toward North Korea, offering to talk with the North, delaying taking the matter to the

UN Security Council, and even intimating, on January 14, 2003, that some combination of economic, food, and energy aid might be considered in combination with security guarantees—but only if North Korea first agreed to give up its nuclear arms program. North Korea rejected the offer, refusing to accept disarmament as a condition for talks. Thereafter, the United States indicated it planned to go to the UN Security Council. The United States also deployed bombers to the northern Pacific, where they would be within easy striking distance, thereby increasing pressure on North Korea.

In early February 2003 U.S. surveillance showed trucks apparently moving spent nuclear fuel rods, causing the United States to fear that the rods might be reprocessed into weaponry. Thereafter, North Korea again increased tensions by announcing that it had reactivated its nuclear facilities, although it promised that its nuclear activity would be limited to peaceful purposes, such as the production of electricity, for the time being. In March 2003 North Korea continued its provocative actions, sending its fighter jets to intercept an unarmed U.S. spy plane on a surveillance mission and test-firing two antiship missiles into the Sea of Japan.

A war of words also ensued. North Korea threatened war if the United States made a preemptive strike on its nuclear facilities. U.S. officials, meanwhile, called North Korea a terrorist nation and a proliferator of missile technology, and threatened a naval blockade to turn back or seize ships and aircraft from North Korea that were suspected of carrying missiles or nuclear weapons materials. In response, North Korea threatened to abandon its commitment to the 1953 armistice that had ended the Korean War. The United States also stated it intended to pursue sanctions against the country at the United Nations, an action that North Korea said it would consider an act of war. Adding to the tension, on the eve of a planned U.S. military strike on Iraq, U.S. defense secretary Donald Rumsfeld warned North Korea not to take advantage of any U.S. action in Iraq, asserting that America would be able to fight and win two regional wars at once.

North Korea's Nuclear Threat

In 1994, in the Agreed Framework negotiated with the United States, North Korea agreed to halt a plutonium weapons program that used spent fuel rods from nuclear power plants to produce nuclear weapons. This agreement idled one nuclear power plant, a plutonium-reprocessing plant, and stopped construction on two other nuclear power plants. In exchange for halting its nuclear power and weapons production, North Korea was promised the type of nuclear power plants called light-water power plants (from which it is difficult to extract plutonium for making weapons) as well as heavy fuel oil for electrical power until the new power plants were built.

A new nuclear crisis unfolded in October 2002 after the United States claimed that North Korea indicated in talks with U.S. assistant secretary of state James Kelly that it was working on a uranium-enrichment nuclear weapons program, a method of producing weapons different from the plutonium program begun in the early 1990s. After the October 2002 announcement of the uranium program, the North also reactivated its plutonium facilities, creating concern because these facilities are already built and could quickly produce enough plutonium for several nuclear bombs. Notably, international observers also believe that North Korea had extracted some plutonium before the 1994 agreement and that it used this plutonium after the agreement to develop nuclear weapons. According to reporter Notra Trulock in an article entitled "North Korea's Nuclear Threat," written for *Insight on the News*, U.S. intelligence reports published in 2001 reveal that "North Korea had produced one, possibly two, nuclear weapons" during the 1990s. Experts therefore believe that the North already possesses nuclear weapons as well as short- and medium-range missiles to deliver them to targets as far away as South Korea and Japan. If North Korea proceeds to reprocess spent fuel rods it could develop six to eight additional nuclear weapons within months, making it a credible nuclear threat in the Asia region. If North Korea continues to develop its missile program, it also could potentially target the United States with nuclear weapons.

Throughout this period, North Korea maintained that it was seeking a diplomatic solution to the crisis. The North consistently demanded bilateral talks with the United States and a nonaggression treaty to end the crisis. For example, Choe Jin Su, North Korea's ambassador to China, stated "If the United States will sign a nonaggression treaty that will have binding force after being ratified by Congress, . . . North Korea has a willingness to prove that it is not making nuclear weapons."[47] The United States ruled out a nonaggression treaty, stating that there was no chance such a treaty would ever win the two-thirds majority in the U.S. Senate needed for congressional confirmation. However, the United States stated it was willing to talk with North Korea but wanted other nations involved in the talks.

South Korea's response to the crisis was to hold talks with the North and offer to mediate discussions with the United States. China and Russia likewise pledged to use their influence to stop North Korea's nuclear weapons development and urged the United States to negotiate. Finally, in April 2003, talks began between North Korea, the U.S., and China, but as of June 2003 the crisis has not been resolved.

North Korea's Nuclear Goals

To many political observers, the 2002–2003 nuclear crisis appeared to be yet another example of North Korea's attempt to

Millions gather in Pyongyang in January 2003 to listen to propaganda praising Kim Jong Il's decision to withdraw from the nuclear nonproliferation treaty.

extort strategic goals from the United States and South Korea. Others say that North Korea has no intention of destroying its nuclear weapons capabilities no matter what agreements are reached, because the otherwise small and weak country believes it needs nuclear weapons to retain its independence and ensure its security in the post–Cold War world.

The 2002–2003 crisis was strikingly similar to North Korea's 1993 threat of nuclear weapons development that spawned the 1994 agreement, except that this time, North Korea asked for peace guarantees instead of economic aid. Specifically, Kim Jong Il demanded talks with the United States to negotiate a nonaggression treaty. This demand, at least on the surface, can be read as a bid for security from U.S. military action against the North Korean regime, with nuclear weapons as leverage.

Despite the confrontational approach, therefore, North Korea's actions may have clear foreign policy goals. As analyst Paul Chamberlin states, North Korea's quite logical goal is to "deter attack by the United States, South Korea, and other countries by developing powerful military capabilities, including WMD [weapons of mass destruction], and pursuing diplomatic solutions with controversial security programs as possible bargaining chips."[48] Another analyst, Derek Mitchell, who worked at the Pentagon on Asia policy during President Bill Clinton's administration, explains: "People talk about North Korea being crazy, but it's not. It's purely rational for a nation with no assets being threatened by the world's major power to develop insurance against attack."[49] In essence, then, it is possible that North Korean leader Kim Jong Il sees increased militarism and development of nuclear and other unconventional weapons and missiles as his best means of self-defense.

Some analysts, however, worry that North Korea's pursuit of nuclear weapons might be for offensive purposes, to carry out its historical goal of forcing a reunification with South Korea under Communist rule. Korean affairs scholar Adrian Buzo, for example, states:

[North Korea] has been developing nuclear weapons in support of its basic three-front strategy for reunification. From Pyongyang's perspective, as the conventional warfare option faded in the 1970s, nuclear weapons became a sheer necessity. If the North were ever to prevail over the South it needed an equaliser against the growing conventional weapons superiority of the South and a means of neutralizing the US nuclear threat. Failure to develop some counter to these two strategic weaknesses would have condemned the DPRK [North Korea] to an unacceptable status of permanent weakness and inferiority.[50]

The Danger of North Korea's Missile Sales

North Korea has become one of the world's most prominent purveyors of missiles; it sells missiles and missile technology to countries which the United States considers to be dangerous, including Iraq, Iran, and Syria. In a 2002 report entitled "Overview of North Korea's Ballistic Missile Program," the Center for Nonproliferation Studies explains the history of North Korea's missile development and sales.

The report explains that North Korea began to develop missiles in the early 1980s to compensate for the lack of a long-range strike capability in its air force. Full-scale production of the Scud-C ballistic missile began in 1991. The North then tested a short-range Nodong-1 ballistic missile in May 1993 (range of about 500 km). Later, longer-range Nodong missiles were produced (range of approximately 1,500 km). Finally, in August 1998, North Korea tested an intermediate-range Taepodong I ballistic missile (range of 3,800 km to 5,900 km). The 1998 missile test confirms that North Korea possesses missiles that can reach not only South Korea, China, and Russia, but also Japan. The launch also shows that North Korea possesses a high degree of technical ability and suggests that it could develop even longer-range missile systems in the future, including missiles with an intercontinental range that could reach the United States.

North Korea, for more than a decade, also has sold missiles and missile technology to other countries. These exports have provided the North with much-needed hard currency. However, as the

Regardless of Kim Jong Il's motivation, what does seem clear to many is that North Korea is committed to building nuclear weapons. Even after the signing of the 1994 framework agreement, experts say the North Korean regime retained enough plutonium for probably two nuclear bombs, and it clearly continued to develop missile technology. Some think the amount of nuclear material is even greater. For example, Lee Wha Rang, an analyst with the Federation of American Scientists, suggests the North may have "close to 10 operational nuclear warheads for its missiles and two nuclear devices that can be carried by truck, boat or transport aircraft."[51]

report describes, the transfer of missile technology creates instability in both Asia and the Middle East, as missile production and sales give countries the ability to threaten their neighbors and pose the risk of regional arms races in those areas.

If such missiles were transferred to Iran, Syria, Pakistan, or Libya, it could trigger off a regional missile race in the Middle East and South Asia.

North Korea's continued development of long-range missiles could also lead to a strategic arms race in Northeast Asia. South Korea is already seeking to develop a 300km-range missile. Indeed, both South Korea and Japan could respond to this impetus by seeking to build a missile defense system. Given the unreliability of current missile defense systems, South Korea and Japan may also find it necessary to develop their own delivery systems to carry out deep strikes within North Korea. Furthermore, in the event of . . . the emergence of a North Korean nuclear capability, South Korea, which had a nuclear weapons program in the 1970s, may go nuclear as well.

Even if the threat posed by North Korea itself is controlled, the export of missile production equipment and the establishment of production facilities in Syria, Iran and Pakistan have already occurred. Thus, the effects of North Korea's production and proliferation of missiles and missile technology promise to extend well into the future.

North Korea also has short- and medium-range missiles (Nodong and Taepodong I) that can reach South Korea and Japan and is known to have been developing others (Taepodong II) that could even reach the United States. In February 2003 the U.S. director of Central Intelligence, George J. Tenet, confirmed that North Korea had completed development of a long-range missile. While testifying before that Senate Armed Services Committee, Tenet was directly asked whether North Korea had a ballistic missile capable of hitting the continental United States; he responded "yes, they can do that."[52]

Other Weapons of Mass Destruction

Some American analysts believe the North has also developed chemical and biological weapons. Experts believe North Korea has been working since the 1960s on developing biological weapons, including smallpox, cholera, yellow fever, typhus, and other viruses. As John R. Bolton, undersecretary of state for arms control and international security, stated in 2002, "North Korea has a dedicated, national-level effort to achieve a biological-weapons capability and has developed and produced, and may have weaponized, biological weapons."[53] In addition, North Korea is believed to have the capacity to produce large amounts of chemical weapons annually, including mustard, phosgene, and sarin. Bolton, for example, cited a defense paper published by the South Korean government, which noted that "North Korea has a minimum of 2,500 tons of lethal chemicals, and that North Korea is 'exerting its utmost efforts to produce chemical weapons.'"[54]

Dangers of a Nuclear North Korea

The reactivation of facilities closed in 1994 would place North Korea in the position of again having the capacity to build nuclear weapons; by restarting its reprocessing center, U.S. officials believe North Korea could produce enough plutonium for four to six more bombs within four months. Thus even if negotiations eventually result in an agreement to stop production, the crisis created by the North could allow it to increase its nuclear weapons stockpile. In addition, if no agreement is reached to stop its nuclear program, North Korea theoretically could also begin selling nuclear weapons for much-needed cash, just as it does missiles and missile technology, a possibility that greatly frightens the United States and the international community concerned already with the spread of weapons of mass destruction.

North Korea's nuclear strategy also serves to divide and increase tensions among surrounding foreign powers and the United States. For example, political analyst Nicholas Eberstadt warns that "Beijing's and Moscow's sharp criticisms of Washington's newly proposed system of 'national missile defense'—a program American policymakers expressly justify

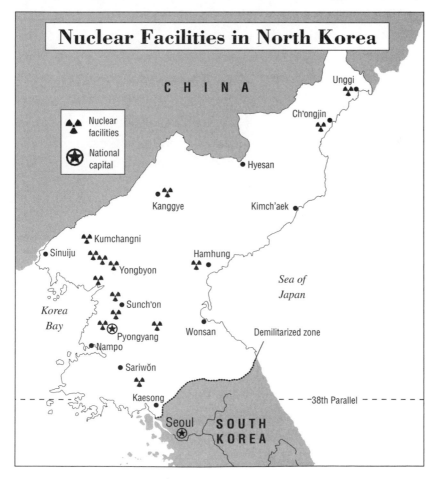

Nuclear Facilities in North Korea

as a shield against the gathering North Korean WMD [weapons of mass destruction] threat—is only a foretaste of such potential tensions."[55] Moreover, there are fears that a nuclear North Korea would start a nuclear arms race in Asia; Japan, in particular, may feel intensely threatened by this development. Further, insistence by the North on keeping its nuclear weapons program may cause the United States to consider a military strike to take out nuclear facilities, a risky proposition given North Korea's threats to retaliate against any such hostile action.

North Korea's Uncertain Future

6

North Korea's future depends on how it responds to the enormous economic and political problems facing the country. Some political observers expect the regime to eventually crumble as external and internal pressures slowly erode the loyalty of North Korea's military leaders to Kim Jong Il; there are signs, such as the defection of military officers, that this may already be happening. On the other hand, some experts see signs that Kim Jong Il's regime wants to initiate free-market economic reforms, pursue peaceful reunification with the South, and make peace with the United States and Japan, in order to stabilize relations with its neighbors. The true intentions of Kim Jong Il and his regime, however, remain unknowable to the outside world.

The Strength of Kim Jong Il's Totalitarian Regime

In the first decade of the twenty-first century, North Korea is an anomaly—a Communist nation surviving despite extreme economic and political pressures in a world where few nations subscribe to communism. Many observers predicted the demise of the North Korean regime after the collapse of the Soviet Union in 1991. Others believed the North Korean government could not survive the death of its leader, Kim Il Sung, in 1994. Still others expected that the economic hardships and mass starvation that afflicted the nation in 1995 and 1996 would lead North Koreans to view the new Kim Jong Il regime as illegitimate and to rise up against him. All these predictions, however, have so far been proven wrong.

Some analysts argue that the longevity of North Korea's regime can be attributed to its unique ideology of *Juche;* as scholar Han S. Park puts it, "the foremost contribution that *Juche* has made to the system is to keep it from collapsing."[56] The *Juche* characteristics that help provide great security for the North Korean regime embody many features of Stalinism, including: a fierce nationalism, a strict adherence to Communist ideology, a system of intense political indoctrination and rigid control of citizenry, a deification of the ruling dictator and class, almost total isolation from the outside world and its ideas or attractions, and an aggressive militarism aimed at discouraging outside interference or influence and procuring benefits to enhance and prolong the regime. These characteristics allow the regime to survive despite economic hardships. As scholar Andrei Lankov states, "The experience of North Korea demonstrates that, in spite of their normally unsatisfactory economic performance, the Stalinist regimes can be very tenacious if they succeed in cutting their populace off from outside influences, are ready to resist foreign pressures stubbornly, and refuse to reform themselves whatever hardships such a decision imposes on the populace."[57]

Prolonging the Regime's Life

Indeed, analysts suggest that as long as the power elite and the military in repressive governments like North Korea's are not severely affected by the economic decline, the regime appears to stay secure. If this is true, the world's humanitarian provision of food and economic aid only strengthens the regime and prolongs its life, because, as American Enterprise Institute analyst Chuck Downs explains, "The regime will determine that food supplies, health services, and commercial investments are provided to those who are loyal and withheld from those who are not."[58] Indeed, North Korea has been observed doing exactly

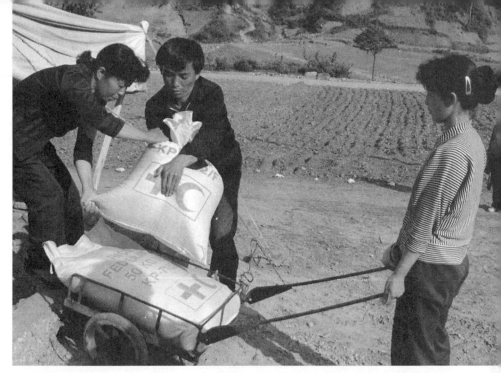

North Korean relief workers prepare food donations for distribution.
Some relief agencies have protested the government's practice of
using aid to reward loyalty to the regime.

this; in 1998 the charitable organization Doctors Without
Borders withdrew its workers from North Korea because the
regime was, it said, "feeding children from families loyal to the
regime while neglecting others."[59]

Since Kim Jong Il's regime has survived despite economic
hardships, experts say the only other sources of danger to the
nation's leadership would be an internal power conflict or a military attack by foreign powers. As for internal regime challenges,
Kim Il Sung managed to eliminate all opposition to his leadership within North Korea throughout his half-century rule; and his
son, Kim Jong Il, by linking himself closely with the Kim Il Sung
cult, has maintained firm control over the country since his suc-
cession. The final threat to the regime, from foreign nations, is
one that Kim Jong Il continually seeks to manage. Political
observers believe that Kim Jong Il considers the United States to
be the most likely aggressor, particularly since U.S. president
Bush's inclusion of North Korea in the "axis of evil."

Regime security thus may provide the best explanation for
North Korea's militarism and pursuit of nuclear and other

weapons of mass destruction. As Han S. Park explains, "The goals of North Korea are not fundamentally different from those of any other system, in that it pursues first and foremost system survival and a stable leadership."[60] Clearly, nuclear weapons provide a powerful deterrent against a U.S. attack, especially if, as the U.S. intelligence officials now conclude, North Korea also has developed a long-range missile that could deliver nuclear weapons to the United States.

Today, most observers expect that the Kim Jong Il regime's *Juche* policies of isolation and militancy will help it to survive in the short run. Many analysts agree, however, that the long-term key to improving both North Korea's economy and its national security is improvement of its relations with countries that can help it acquire loans and economic assistance and help it integrate into the international community. As *Time* magazine's Donald Macintyre states, the "devastating famine in the mid-'90s made it clear [North Korea] could not go it alone—that it must, to some degree, join the international economic community."[61] Ultimately, therefore, to reverse the economic decline, the regime may have to change its *Juche* policies.

Hwang Jang Yop was a high-ranking North Korean government official before defecting to South Korea in 1997.

Defections and Dissent

There have been some signs of dissatisfaction at home with the North Korean regime, most notably a number of defections of North Koreans to South Korea. The most famous example is the defection on February 12, 1997, of Hwang Jang Yop, a high-ranking government official who, unlike most North Koreans, was allowed to travel abroad. His defection for many observers signaled a clear weakening of the North Korean regime, because Hwang is famous for being the main architect of North Korea's core *Juche* ideology. Hwang, shortly after his defection to Seoul, South Korea, held a news conference, where he confirmed that the support of North Koreans for Kim Jong Il is weak:

> You are asking how much the North Korean people support Kim Jong Il and how stable North Korea is, correct? Well, I cannot express in words how the people support or oppose him. Since the North Korean leadership blocks the people's ears, eyes, and mouths; shackles their feet; and prevents their free movement, the North Korean people cannot express themselves. There is no freedom of expression in North Korean society. However, I think most of those who are aware of the external situation do not support Kim Jong Il. If Kim Jong Il commanded extensive and wide support, he would not say that the only organ he can trust is the army. All North Koreans have their ears, eyes, and mouths closed; but the eyes, ears, and mouths of the army are more completely closed than any other group. Kim Jong Il's remark that he can trust only the army means he cannot trust the people. However, in North Korea, those who rise up against Kim Jong Il cannot sustain themselves. We cannot say there are people who are united around such dissidents, as some might think. Why would hundreds of thousands of people have gone to the national security department and got themselves killed? Therefore, you should not think that the people support him because they cannot hold demonstrations and strikes like they can here. That society is fundamentally different from society here. It is a society which cannot be seen in any other country of the world.[62]

South Korean President Roh Moo Hyun's Policies on North Korea

On December 19, 2002, South Korea elected a new president to replace Kim Dae Jung, architect of the South's "Sunshine Policy" toward North Korea. This policy favors peaceful negotiations and engagement with the North to improve relations between the two countries and eventually move toward reunification of the Korean peninsula. Some South Koreans had grown disillusioned with the "Sunshine Policy" after the 2000 summit between North and South Korean leaders failed to produce substantial improvement in relations. Many expected the conservative presidential candidate to win the presidential election.

Instead, South Koreans elected Roh Moo Hyun, a lawyer and human-rights advocate who favors continued engagement with North Korea. He promises to continue Kim Dae Jung's "Sunshine Policy" toward the North and to bring peace to the Korean peninsula. Roh Moo Hyun's approach to the 2002–2003 nuclear crisis in North Korea is to seek peaceful resolution through dialogue. He urges North Korea and the United States to work out an agreement in which the North agrees to stop production of weapons of mass destruction and accept international inspections in exchange for an international economic aid package.

Although Roh Moo Hyun has stated that he has no plans to abandon South Korea's ties with the United States, his engagement approach to the North creates tensions with the United States, because the administration of U.S. president George W. Bush has adopted more conservative views. In preliminary talks with the United States, for example, representatives of Roh Moo Hyun indicated that South Korea would oppose punitive actions which the United States had considered against North Korea, such as sanctions or military strikes. Roh Moo Hyun later publicly confirmed that he opposes any consideration of an armed attack on North Korea; this option, he said, could start a war. Roh Moo Hyun took office on February 25, 2003.

South Korean president Roh Moo Hyun wishes to improve relations with North Korea.

Hwang is on record as saying that "the minds of the general public are slowly deserting the system in favor of reform";[63] as proof, he points to the fact that North Koreans accused of speech or actions against the regime's policies now often refuse to renounce their beliefs as they did in the past.

In addition to Hwang Yang Yop, a steady stream of other defectors have left North Korea, including government and military officials as well as ordinary citizens. Between 1997 and 1998, for example, an army officer, Captain Byon Yong Kwan, and several government officials—Kim Dong Su, the third secretary in North Korea's diplomatic mission to the Rome headquarters of the UN Food and Agriculture Organization; Jang Sung Gil, North Korea's ambassador to Egypt; and Jang Sung Ho, a trade official based in Paris—defected.

As analyst Chuck Downs notes, "there is an increasing flow of ordinary working people who are willing to risk their lives for nothing more than a chance to move their families away from North Korea."[64] Often, these escapees flee across the border to China, where they are quietly assisted by the Chinese in traveling to other countries. Although many are escaping hunger and economic problems, this flow of refugees also appears to reflect a deep dissatisfaction with North Korea, given the harsh penalties people face if they are captured. Those who are apprehended by North Korean authorities are forced to return to North Korea where, as authors Nicolette Jackson and Sean Healy have documented, they "face a minimum seven years' detention, forced labour and torture in a reform institution; in 'extremely grave' cases, they face the death penalty."[65] Another witness states that in some cases "the North Korean police put a metal wire through the noses of some people who escape, like a brand that marks them out."[66]

Signs of Economic Reform

Faced with so many economic problems, North Korea in the late 1980s and the 1990s showed some signs that it wants to improve its economy, test free-market theories, and modernize along the lines of the Chinese economic model. The North's economic reform efforts, however, have been very cautious.

The North's first major step toward economic reform came in 1984 when it enacted its first Joint Venture Law. As scholar Samuel S. Kim states, "Modeled after China's open-door policy and legislation, [North Korea] wishfully targeted a three-fold increase in exports for its Third Seven-Year Plan (1987–93)."[67] In 1992 North Korea enacted three sets of new laws to encourage foreign investment: the Foreigners Investment Law of the DPRK, the Contractual Joint Venture Law of the DPRK, and the Law of the DPRK on Foreign Enterprises. These laws were designed to make it easier for foreign companies to do business in and with North Korea.

Results, however, have been disappointing. Western firms consider ventures with North Korea highly risky due mostly to the country's shaky credit status but also to other factors such as the country's international political problems, its attitude of suspicion toward other countries, its lack of experience in capitalist economic ventures, and the lack of clear regulations and procedures governing for foreign investments. Capitalist ventures that have been attempted have not survived; for example, a venture called the Tumen River Area Development Project, designed to open up new trade routes to the Chinese and Russians, was abandoned seven years later. In large part, the initiatives have only encouraged South Koreans and Japanese-Koreans to invest in North Korea rather than Western nations. In 1998, for example, North Korea entered into a $942 million deal with South Korea's Hyundai Group allowing it to bring tourists from South Korea to North Korea's Mount Kumgang, just north of the DMZ; Hyundai lost money in the deal and eventually sought a bailout from the South Korean government, although tours continue.

North Korea also has received technical assistance from the UN Committee for Trade and Development (UNCTAD) to help it develop an international trade strategy. UNCTAD sought to improve North Korea's knowledge in three areas:

foreign trade, exports, and the creation of free economic and export zones. The government of North Korea, however, placed limits on the UNCTAD consulting efforts and made it clear that it envisioned only partial reforms. As a result of this reluctance to embrace reform, North Korea's economy is less able to respond to economic challenges and developments. As economists and consultants Frederick Nixson and Paul Collins explain, "Decision makers in both government and state trading enterprises are insufficiently informed and lack the experience of flexible response to quickly changing situations. All kinds of constraints—marketing, credit, transport, insurance—inhibit rapid transformations."[68]

Moving from a Communist Economy

In July 2002, however, North Korea undertook what outsiders view as a major step in moving from a Communist economy to a free-market economy. The state began moving wages and prices, which had long been dictated by the government, closer to market levels, phasing out state economic controls such as state subsidies for industries and ration coupons that North Koreans use to pay for food, clothing, and other staples. These actions are similar to the changes that China pursued in the early days of its economic modernization program in the 1970s, but whether North Korea's experience with market reforms will mirror China's is an open question. The regime so far has refused to explain or even announce the new policies, making it difficult for outsiders to assess their true potential or their results.

A central problem, however, with all of North Korea's economic schemes is the country's huge foreign debt and lack of a good credit rating—a problem that dates back to the North's attempt in 1972 to improve productivity by importing Western industrial technologies and equipment. The government defaulted on its obligations and by 1989 was burdened by billions of dollars worth of foreign debt. As analyst Samuel S. Kim states, North Korea thus is caught in "a catch-22 bind: A successful export strategy is not possible without massive

The China Model for North Korea's Economic Reforms

In the 1970s China was facing economic problems similar to those currently facing North Korea. It, too, was having difficulties feeding its people. In response, Chinese leader Teng Hsiao-p'ing in 1978 introduced the first elements of a market economy. China's economic reform plan became known as the "four modernizations" (in industry, agriculture, science, and defense). It included (1) ending the system of collective agriculture and letting farmers sell their own produce; (2) opening China to foreign trade, technology, and investment; (3) seeking better diplomatic relations with Western countries such as the United States; and (4) relaxing the Maoist/Communist ideology to allow expanded political, social, and cultural freedoms.

Kim Jong Il visited China in 2000 and 2001 to view the effects of China's reforms, and seemed interested in implementing some form of similar reforms in North Korea. North Korea has enacted several legislative measures designed to encourage foreign investment, has designated several areas as special economic zones to promote for-profit business ventures, and in July 2002 began to raise wages and prices of goods to stimulate free-market forces in the North Korean economy. Both China and South Korea appear interested in helping the North modernize its economy, and better relations with the United States would assist North Korea in obtaining crucial international loans to aid in the purchase of technology and equipment.

imports of high-tech equipment and plants, which in turn would not be possible without hard-currency credits, which in turn would not be possible without first paying off its foreign debts through a successful export strategy and so on in a vicious circle."[69]

Diplomatic Overtures

Experts say the key to solving North Korea's economic problems lies in improving its relationships with long-time adversaries such as the United States and Japan, which can help the country get loans from the international community through sources such as the World Bank and the International Monetary Fund. Perhaps toward this end, Kim Jong Il in recent years has initiated a number of diplomatic efforts to improve his country's relationships with the rest of the world.

In 1999, for example, Kim Jong Il made efforts to reestablish or strengthen relationships with China, Russia, and Japan. In 2000 he met with South Korean president Kim Dae Jung in the now-famous summit; indeed, the summit led to many benefits for the North, including aid and various economic ventures, and it inspired the United States to partially lift U.S. trade sanctions. After the summit, North Korea joined the ASEAN Regional Forum, a regional security organization, and applied for membership in the Asian Development Bank, an international financial organization. Kim Jong Il also received Russian president Vladimir Putin for a visit in 2000 and established diplomatic relationships with Italy, Australia, the Philippines, Great Britain, the Netherlands, Belgium, Canada, Spain, Germany, and others. In addition, North Korea tried to improve relations with the United States, meeting with Secretary of State Madeleine Albright in October 2000, and

North Korean leader Kim Jong Il (right) joins hands with South Korean president Kim Dae Jung at the June 2000 summit meeting.

seeking but failing to meet with U.S. president Clinton when a missile deal could not be finalized.

Since the new century dawned, North Korea has continued its diplomatic efforts. Kim Jong Il made two visits to China in 2000 and 2001. China provides a model for North Korea to undertake economic restructuring without changing its Communist government, and during his visits Kim Jong Il witnessed firsthand the success of China's market-based economic reforms. Today China, more than any other country, also provides North Korea economic support in the form of direct financial and food aid. In 2002, in another historic summit, Kim Jong Il met with Japan's prime minister, Junichiro Koizumi. The talks resulted in an admission by North Korea that it abducted eleven Japanese citizens during the Cold War to act as language instructors, an apology from Japan for its colonization and wartime conduct in Korea, and a package of billions of dollars of aid to North Korea. Also in 2002, North Korea participated in its first-ever international sports event, the fourteenth Asian Games, where teams from North and South Korea marched together at the opening ceremony under one flag.

Continuing Provocative Tendencies

Many of these attempts at diplomacy, however, have encountered difficulties, often due to North Korea's continuing provocative tendencies. For example, the talks with Japan resulted in North Korea's agreement to indefinitely extend its moratorium on testing long-range missiles, leading the United States to agree to send a delegation to North Korea in October 2002. When the North finally acquired a meeting with the Americans, however, it announced it was again developing nuclear weapons, thereby confirming right-wing American beliefs that the regime cannot be trusted. Also, after the Japan summit, North Korea permitted five of the original eleven abducted Japanese to visit Japan and provided remains of those who had died, but this goodwill gesture backfired when Japan learned that the remains of one victim, who supposedly died in North Korea, were actually those of someone else, raising

North Korea's Kidnapping of Japanese Citizens

North Korea has long been accused of a series of kidnappings of Japanese citizens—particularly young couples—from along the Japan Sea coast beginning in 1978. On September 17, 2002, North Korean leader Kim Jong Il met with Japanese prime minister Junichiro Koizumi in Pyongyang, North Korea, in a historic summit. During the summit, North Korea admitted to kidnapping eleven Japanese citizens to act as language instructors during the Cold War.

In a May 3, 1997, analysis entitled "Why North Korea Kidnapped Japanese Citizens," Sato Katsumi, director of the Modern Korea Institute, explains the details of why North Korea kidnapped the Japanese couples. He points out that North Korea wanted to train its agents to pose as Japanese, speak Japanese, and carry forged Japanese passports in terrorist activities against South Korea. This, according to Katsumi, satisfied several North Korean goals:

> It would be easier for North Korean terrorists to operate if they carried forged passports which made them appear Japanese, as Japan enjoys a high level of trust internationally. Furthermore, even if a North Korean terrorist carrying such a passport happened to fail in carrying out his mission, the blame would be placed on a Japanese rather than attributed to North Korea, and thus North Korea would be protected from damage. Meanwhile, relations between Japan and South Korea would be harmed. In any case the net result would be a weakening of the South Korean government. This line of thinking—the use of "apparently Japanese" terrorists carrying forged Japanese passports—appealed greatly to the KWP as it seemed that several birds could be felled with one stone. Given the timing of events, it is hypothesized that the KWP decided to adopt a policy of kidnapping Japanese and using them in terrorist activities.

North Korea, in the 2002 summit with Japan, promised to allow kidnapped Japanese to return home to Japan. Although the North permitted Japanese kidnap victims to travel to Japan and sent the remains of some Japanese who had died in North Korea, the Japanese discovered that the remains of one victim, Kaoru Matsuki, who supposedly died in North Korea at age forty-two, were those of a sixty-year-old woman. This suggests that North Korea had been deceptive about explaining the deaths of some of the Japanese victims.

suspicions that North Korea likely had deceived Japan. Even North Korea's relations with China have become strained over the numbers of North Korean refugees streaming into China.

Also, despite North Korea's experiments with economic reform and its outreach to other countries, the regime seems deeply reluctant to risk the increased exposure to the outside world that true reform would bring. As recently as May 2000, the official newspaper published by the Korean Workers' Party published an article that argued: "If one wants the prosperity of the national economy, he should thoroughly reject the idea of dependence on outside forces, the idea that he cannot live without foreign capital. . . . We must heighten vigilance against the imperialists' moves to induce us to 'Reform' and 'opening to the outside world.' 'Reform' and 'opening' on their lips are a honey-coated poison."[70]

Moreover, attracting foreign investment necessary for economic recovery requires North Korea to normalize relations with countries with which it has a very troubled history, such as South Korea, Japan, and the United States. North Korea thus is caught between needing radical economic reform and the risk that such reform will destabilize its regime, and between needing to build trust with foreign countries and its continuing pattern of manipulating and threatening them as military enemies.

Epilogue
North Korea in the Post–Cold War World

North Korea has yet to find a place for itself in the post-Communist world. With the end of the Cold War, the dynamics of Asia and the world powers have changed, creating a reordered set of relationships and the possibility of increased cooperation among the various powers. North Korea, meanwhile, remains relatively isolated from other nations, increasingly militarist, its future unstable due to its unsolved economic problems and continuing provocative behavior.

The new relationships among world powers such as China, Japan, and the United States reflect a trend toward globalization and economic cooperation in Asia. China's embrace of capitalist economic reforms has improved its relations with the West and enhanced its economic power in the Pacific region. Similarly, U.S. allies Japan and South Korea both have grown in both economic and political power in the region and have formed closer economic relationships with each other and with China. Whether the North can integrate into the growing trend toward globalization and economic cooperation in the Asian-Pacific area remains an open question.

Part of the problem, according to scholar Han S. Park, is that because of centuries-old Korean fear of domination by outsiders combined with memories of the Korean War and Cold War, North Korea today continues to see itself as "surrounded by hostile and evil forces that are undermining its legitimacy."[71] To Kim Jong Il and his followers, these forces include the United States, South Korea, and Japan. In North Korea's view, not only do these countries still represent potential military threats; they also advocate reforms for the North that the regime fears could cause its system to collapse. The challenge for Kim Jong Il, therefore, is how to ensure the security of his regime while at the

Protesters in Seoul demand an end to North Korea's nuclear weapons development program.

same time opening the country to economic reforms, attracting foreign investors, and normalizing relations with foreign countries.

Meanwhile, the dilemma for policy makers is how to discern Kim Jong Il's true intentions and whether to view North Korea as a country that can exist peacefully in the world community or as a dangerous pariah. The world's response to the 2002 nuclear crisis engendered by North Korea's resumption of nuclear weapons development illustrates, at the very least, that the interests of all the great powers converge with respect to North Korea. The United States, China, Russia, South Korea, and Japan all want to see a stable and denuclearized Korean peninsula. Disagreements have emerged, however, on how to achieve this goal. China, historically tied to the Communist North and provider of a significant amount of the food aid that keeps the regime afloat, refrains from actively pressuring Kim Jong Il and seems committed to preventing the collapse of the country. Similarly, South Korea favors policies of engagement and fears an economic collapse that could destabilize the Korean peninsula or negatively affect its economic prosperity. Japan, for its part, fears military attack from

North Korea and has tried to normalize relations, while Russia mainly seeks stability in the region. The United States, after attempting to engage the North in the 1990s, currently views the country as a "rogue" state that cannot be trusted and remains skeptical of engagement policies.

Although most signs indicate that diplomacy, not military action, will be employed by the world powers to contain North Korean militarism, the success of such efforts in restraining Kim Jong Il and his response to incentives designed to convince him to let North Korea join the international community cannot now be predicted.

Notes

Chapter One: North Korea's Beginnings: The Cold War Division of Korea

1. Don Oberdorfer, *The Two Koreas*. New York: Basic Books, 2001, p. 3.

2. Takashi Hatada, *A History of Korea*. Santa Barbara, CA: ABC-Clio, 1969, p. 115.

3. Quoted in Bruce Cumings, *Korea's Place in the Sun*. New York: W.W. Norton, 1997, p. 159.

4. Quoted in Koon Woo Nam, *The North Korean Communist Leadership, 1945–1965*. Tuscaloosa: University of Alabama Press, 1974, p. 14.

5. Quoted in Geoff Simons, *Korea: The Search for Sovereignty*. New York: St. Martin's, 1995, p. 159.

6. Cumings, *Korea's Place in the Sun*, p. 10.

Chapter Two: Communist North Korea

7. Koon Woo Nam, *The North Korean Communist Leadership, 1945–1965*, pp. 140–41.

8. Cumings, *Korea's Place in the Sun*, p. 404.

9. Koon Woo Nam, *The North Korean Communist Leadership, 1945–1965*, p. 126.

10. Andrei Lankov, *From Stalin to Kim Il Sung*. London: Hurst, 2002, p. 195.

11. Ilpyong J. Kim, *Communist Politics in North Korea*. New York: Praeger, 1975, p. 109.

12. Quoted in Andrea Matles Savada, ed., *North Korea: A Country Study*. Washington, DC: Library of Congress, 1994, p. 151.

13. Quoted in Koon Woo Nam, *The North Korean Communist Leadership, 1945–1965*, p. 127.

14. Simons, *Korea: The Search for Sovereignty*, p. 231.

15. Quoted in Hazel Smith et al., eds., *North Korea in the New World Order*. New York: St. Martin's, 1996, p. 156.

16. Quoted in Koon Woo Nam, *The North Korean Communist Leadership, 1945–1965*, p. 130.

17. Simons, *Korea: The Search for Sovereignty*, pp. 241–42.

Chapter Three: North Korea's Military and Foreign Policy

18. Chuck Downs, *Over the Line: North Korea's Negotiating Strategy*. Washington, DC: AIE Press, 1999, p. 117.

19. Koon Woo Nam, *The North Korean Communist Leadership, 1945–1965*, pp. 145–46.

20. Oberdorfer, *The Two Koreas*, p. 103.

21. Quoted in Downs, *Over the Line*, p. 165.

22. Downs, *Over the Line*, p. 2.

23. Quoted in Savada, *North Korea,* p. 262.

24. Quoted in Savada, *North Korea,* p. 262.

25. Downs, *Over the Line*, p. 196.

26. Quoted in Downs, *Over the Line*, p. 181.

27. Cumings, *Korea's Place in the Sun*, p. 467.

28. Downs, *Over the Line*, p. 239.

29. Quoted in Downs, *Over the Line*, p. 250.

Chapter Four: The 1990s: A Time of Challenges

30. Daniel Goodkind and Loraine West, "The North Korean Famine and Its Demographic Impact," *Population and Development Review*, June 2001.

31. Quoted in Simons, *Korea: The Search for Sovereignty*, p. 243.

32. Han S. Park, *North Korea: The Politics of Unconventional Wisdom.* Boulder, CO: Lynne Rienner, 2002, p. 151.

33. Goodkind and West, "The North Korean Famine and Its Demographic Impact."

34. Oberdorfer, *The Two Koreas*, p. 370.

35. Oberdorfer, *The Two Koreas*, p. 371.

36. Goodkind and West, "The North Korean Famine and Its Demographic Impact."

37. Oberdorfer, *The Two Koreas*, p. 386.

38. Quoted in Oberdorfer, *The Two Koreas*, p. 407.

Chapter Five: North Korea and Weapons of Mass Destruction

39. George W. Bush, "President's State of the Union Address," Washington, DC, January 29, 2002. www.whitehouse.gov.

40. Bush, "President's State of the Union Address."

41. Quoted in *Time*, "How Dangerous Is North Korea?" January 13, 2003.

42. Quoted in *Arms Control Today*, "Progress and Challenges in Denuclearizing North Korea," May 2002.

43. United Press International, "N. Korea Blasts U.S. Nuclear Strategy," March 13, 2002.

44. Quoted in Paul Kerr, "U.S. Sends Conflicting Signals on North Korea," *Arms Control Today*, September 2002.

45. Quoted in Johanna McGeary, "Look Who's Got the Bomb," *Time*, October 28, 2002.

46. Associated Press, "North Korea's Official Radio Backs Off Nuke Report," November 15, 2002.

47. Quoted in Erik Eckholm, "North Korea Presses Demand for Direct Talks with U.S.," *New York Times*, January 31, 2003.

48. Paul Chamberlin, "A Realistic U.S. Policy," *World & I*, January 2003.

49. Quoted in *Time*, "How Dangerous Is North Korea?"

50. Adrian Buzo, *The Guerrilla Dynasty*. Boulder, CO: Westview, 1999, p. 229.

51. Lee Wha Rang, "N. Korea Nuclear Arsenal," Federation of American Scientists. www.kimsoft.com.

52. Quoted in Cable News Network, "Tenet: North Korea Has Ballistic Missile Capable of Hitting U.S.," February 12, 2003. www.cnn.com.

53. Quoted in Marc Lerner, "North Korea Weapons a 'Nuclear Nightmare,'" *Washington Times*, January 17, 2003.

54. John R. Bolton, speech in Seoul, South Korea, August 29, 2002. Office of International Information Programs, U.S. Department of State. http://usinfo.state.gov.

55. Nicholas Eberstadt and Richard J. Ellings, eds., *Korea's Future and the Great Powers*. Seattle: University of Washington Press, 2001, p. 13.

Chapter Six: North Korea's Uncertain Future
56. Park, *North Korea*, p. 161.

57. Lankov, *From Stalin to Kim Il Sung*, pp. 196–97.

58. Downs, *Over the Line*, p. 279.

59. Quoted in Downs, *Over the Line*, p. 279.

60. Park, *North Korea*, p. 149.

61. Donald Macintyre, "Light from the North?" *Time International*, August 19, 2002.

62. Quoted in Korea Web Weekly, "July 10 Hwang Jang Yop Press Conference." www.kimsoft.com.

63. Quoted in Downs, *Over the Line*, p. 258.

64. Downs, *Over the Line*, p. 259.

65. Nicolette Jackson and Sean Healy, "Desperate Escape: The Backbreaking Work of North Korean Women," *New Internationalist*, September 2002.

66. Quoted in Downs, *Over the Line*, p. 259.

67. Samuel S. Kim, "North Korea and the Non-Communist World: The Quest for National Identity," in Chong-Sik and Se-He Yoo, eds., *North Korea in Transition*. Berkeley: University of California Press, 1991, p. 37.

68. Frederick Nixson and Paul Collins, "Economic Reform in North Korea," in Smith et al., eds., *North Korea in the New World Order*, p. 163.

69. Kim, "North Korea and the Non-Communist World: The Quest for National Identity," in Chong-Sik and Se-He Yoo, eds., *North Korea in Transition*, p. 37.

70. Quoted in Eberstadt and Ellings, *Korea's Future and the Great Powers*, pp. 196–97.

Epilogue: North Korea in the Post–Cold War World
71. Park, *North Korea*, p. 145.

Chronology

ca. 1100–108 B.C.
The state of ancient Choson rules on the Korean peninsula.

108
The Han Chinese rule on the Korean peninsula.

A.D. 300s
The three kingdoms develop on the Korean peninsula (Paekche, Koguryo, and Silla).

936–1392
The Koryo dynasty rules Korea.

1392–1910
The Choson or Yi dynasty rules Korea.

1895
Japan wins war with China and, in the Treaty of Shimonoseki, China recognizes the independence of Korea, giving Japan greater influence over the area.

1910
Japan officially annexes Korea.

1919
Mass protests of Japan's colonization of Korea known as the March First Movement occur throughout Korea.

1945
Korea is freed from Japanese occupation after Japan is defeated in World War II; Korea is occupied by Russia in the North and the United States in the South.

1947
The United Nations votes to sponsor elections in Korea over Russian objections.

1948

On September 9 the Democratic People's Republic of Korea (DPRK) is proclaimed in North Korea.

1950

On June 25 the Korean War begins when North Korean troops invade South Korea.

1953

The Korean War ends with an armistice agreement on July 27; no formal peace treaty is signed, and North and South Korea remain technically at war.

1956

Kim Il Sung announces a three-year plan of economic development and completes it ahead of schedule.

1961

North Korea signs military assistance treaties with China and the Soviet Union.

1962

North Korea acquires a small two-megawatt nuclear reactor from the Soviet Union.

1972

Kim Il Sung attempts to improve North Korea's sagging economy by importing Western industrial technologies and equipment and begins new economic campaigns.

1976

North Korean guards without provocation attack a group of UN security workers who were pruning a tree at a UN checkpoint in the DMZ

1979

North and South Korea agree to talks, but no progress is made.

1983

In October North Korean agents attempt to assassinate South Korean president Chun Doo Hwan.

1985

North Korea signs the nuclear nonproliferation treaty (NPT), promising not to develop or obtain nuclear weapons.

1987

North Korea completes construction of a thirty-megawatt, gas-graphite nuclear reactor.

1988

In August, North Korea launches a medium-range multistage Taepodong I missile across Japan and into the Pacific Ocean, creating international concern.

1989

The United States detects evidence that North Korea is developing nuclear weapons.

1991

The Soviet Union, one of North Korea's most important allies and economic supporters, collapses.

1992

In January North Korea signs a follow-up implementing agreement for the NPT, permitting international inspections of nuclear facilities.

1994

On October 21 North Korea and the United States sign the Agreed Framework, in which North Korea promises to halt its development of nuclear weapons in return for aid in building civilian nuclear reactors and temporary oil supplies.

1995

Floods afflict North Korea, causing agricultural losses and food shortages.

1996

More flooding occurs, and serious food shortages continue in North Korea, reaching famine proportions.

1998

The food shortages became critical because of a drought that followed the earlier floods; on August 31 North Korea launches a multistage rocket over Japan.

1999

In June North Korea initiates a naval clash with South Korea patrols, leading to a gun battle in which the South sinks a North Korean torpedo boat and its crew.

2000

On June 13–15 North Korean leader Kim Jong Il and South Korean president Kim Dae Jong meet for a summit in Pyongyang and sign a joint declaration pledging to work for reunification.

2002

On January 29, 2002, U.S. president George W. Bush announces in his State of the Union Address that North Korea is part of an "axis of evil" (along with Iraq and Iran); on October 4 North Korea announces that it is developing nuclear weapons.

2003

On January 10 North Korea says it is pulling out of the NPT; on February 5 North Korea announces that it has reactivated its nuclear facilities but promises that its nuclear activity will be limited to peaceful purposes; on February 27 North Korea restarts a reactor in its nuclear facilities.

For Further Reading

Books

Tai Sung An, *North Korea: A Political Handbook*. Wilmington, DE: Scholarly Resources, 1983. This book provides information on North Korea's government and leadership, including biographies of North Korean leaders and an appendix containing the country's constitution and the charter of the Korean Workers' Party.

Michael Breen, *The Koreans: Who They Are, What They Want, Where Their Future Lies*. New York: St. Martin's, 1999. This book discusses contemporary Korea, both North and South Korea, including prospects for reunification.

Carter J. Eckert et al., *Korea Old and New*. Seoul, Korea: Ilchokak, 1990. This is a general history of Korea that focuses on Korea's past century and also provides a detailed treatment of the post-1945 period.

Han Woo-Keun, *The History of Korea*. Seoul, Korea: Eul-Yoo, 1970. This book is a classic history of the Korean peninsula and ancient Korea but does not cover contemporary North Korea.

Donald Stone Macdonald, *The Koreans: Contemporary Politics and Society*. Boulder, CO: Westview, 1996. This book provides a good review of Korean history and culture as well as chapters comparing modern North and South Korean economies, governments, and foreign relations.

Stanley Sandier, *The Korean War: No Victors, No Vanquished*. Lexington: University Press of Kentucky, 1999. This book provides a good history and analysis of the Korean War and its effects on Korea and the world.

Periodicals

Yinhay Ahn, "North Korea in 2001: At a Crossroads," *Asian Survey*, January/February 2002.

David Albright and Holly Higgins, "North Korea: It's Taking Too Long: Inspections in North Korea Are Tied to the Reactor Deal, Which Is Far Behind Schedule," *Bulletin of the Atomic Scientists*, January/February 2002.

Bulletin of the Atomic Scientists, "Letter from Pyongyang," July/August 2002.

Business Week, "The Two Koreas: What's Behind a Break in the Ice," April 15, 2002.

Victor D. Cha, "North Korea's Weapons of Mass Destruction: Badges, Shields, or Swords?" *Political Science Quarterly*, Summer 2002.

Howard G. Chua-Eoan, "The Last Hard-Liner: Kim Il Sung, 1912–1994," *Time*, July 18, 1994.

Stan Crock, "Why Bush Must Talk to Pyongyang," *Business Week Online*, October 25, 2002.

Bruce Cumings, "Endgame in Korea," *Nation*, November 18, 2002.

———, "Summitry in Pyongyang," *Nation*, July 10, 2000.

Michael Duffy and Nancy Gibbs, "When Evil Is Everywhere: Has Bush Been Right All Along, or Is His World View Part of the Problem?" *Time*, Oct 28, 2002.

Economist (US), "Don't Get Too Capitalist, Comrade; China and North Korea," October 12, 2002.

———, "A Friendly Word: China, Russia and North Korea," December 7, 2002.

———, "Getting the Genie Back into the Bottle; North Korea's Nuclear Programme," October 26, 2002.

———, "Needing Refuge; North Koreans in China," June 22, 2002.

———, "Open Sesame—Open Sesame," July 27, 2002.

————, "Stitch by Stitch to a Different World; Free-Market Stirrings in North Korea," July 27, 2002.

Kristen Eichensehr, "Broken Promises," *Harvard International Review*, Fall 2001.

Mel Gurtov, "Common Security in North Korea: Quest for a New Paradigm in Inter-Korean Relations," *Asian Survey*, May/June 2002.

Thomas H. Henrikson, "The Rise and Decline of Rogue States," *Vital Speeches*, March 1, 2001.

Daryl G. Kimball, "Disarmament Through Diplomacy," *Arms Control Today*, November 2002.

Tae-Hwan Kwak and Seung-Ho Joo, "The Korean Peace Process: Problems and Prospects After the Summit," *World Affairs*, Fall 2002.

Angela McFeeters, "Dear Leader Wants His Visa (Card)," *Business Asia*, June 2002.

Nation, "Axis of Incoherence," January 27, 2003.

National Review, "North Korea: Proliferation," November 11, 2002.

Don Oberdorfer, "Better Start Talking—and Fast," *Time*, January 13, 2003.

Thomas Omestad and Mark Mazzetti, "North Korea Breaks a No-Nukes Deal," *U.S. News & World Report*, October 28, 2002.

Progressive, "Axis to Grind," March 2002.

Sharif M. Shuja, "Coping with the 'Axis of Evil,'" *Contemporary Review*, May 2002.

Hideko Takayama, "From Korea with Love," *Newsweek International*, July 8, 2002.

Jonathan Watts, "Balancing the 'Axis of Evil' in Northeast Asia," *Lancet*, September 7, 2002.

George Wehrfritz et al., "Hands Across the Sea," *Newsweek International*, September 16, 2002.

Websites

Asian Info (www.asianinfo.org). This website is dedicated to introducing Asian culture, traditions, and general information to the world.

Federation of American Scientists (www.fas.org). The Federation of American Scientists is a nonprofit organization founded in 1945 by scientists involved in the Manhattan Project, creators of the atom bomb who were concerned about the implications of its use for the future of humankind. The website gives information about nuclear proliferation in Korea.

Korean News Service (www.kcna.co.jp). This is the website for the Korean Central News Agency, a state-run agency of the Democratic People's Republic of Korea. It speaks for the Korean Workers' Party and the DPRK government.

Korea Web Weekly (www.kimsoft.com). This is an independent, nonpartisan, nonprofit website on all things Korean: history, culture, economy, politics, and military, since 1995.

One World (www.oneworld.net). One World is a community of over fifteen hundred organizations working for social justice. This website offers multiple articles chosen from around the world about North Korea. It focuses on events and issues that have developed during the last five years.

U.S. Central Intelligence Agency (CIA) (www.cia.gov). This is a U.S. government website for the CIA, providing geographical, political, economic, and other information on the country of North Korea.

U.S. Department of Energy (www.eia.doe.gov). This is a U.S. government website for the Department of Energy, providing energy-related information about North Korea.

Washington Post (www.washingtonpost.com). This website is for a major American newspaper published in Washington, D.C., that provides up-to-date news on events in North Korea.

Works Consulted

Books

Adrian Buzo, *The Guerilla Dynasty*. Boulder, CO: Westview, 1999. Buzo provides an accessible description of North Korea's political, economic, and foreign policy, demonstrating the connection between North Korean policies and the guerrilla mindset of Kim Il Sung and his followers.

Bruce Cumings, *Korea's Place in the Sun*. New York: W.W. Norton, 1997. This is a history of modern North Korea from its ancient beginnings into the 1990s, written by a well-known authority on the country who often has been critical of U.S. policy toward North Korea.

Chuck Downs, *Over the Line: North Korea's Negotiating Strategy*. Washington, DC: AIE Press, 1999. This is a detailed analysis of North Korea's negotiating style from the end of the Korean War to the late 1990s, written by an associate director of the Asian Studies Program at the American Enterprise Institute, a conservative think tank located in Washington, D.C.

Nicholas Eberstadt and Richard J. Ellings, eds., *Korea's Future and the Great Powers*. Seattle: University of Washington Press, 2001. This book provides a collection of essays addressing the interests of the four great powers—Russia, China, Japan, and the United States—in the Korean peninsula, and covers issues such as strategies for resolving North Korea's economic problems and options for negotiating a reunification of the two Koreas.

Takashi Hatada, *A History of Korea*. Santa Barbara, CA: ABC-Clio, 1969. A classic history of Korea, this book covers Korea's history up to the Korean War and the creation of two separate Koreas, and is written by a Japanese scholar and historian.

Ilpyong J. Kim, *Communist Politics in North Korea.* New York: Praeger, 1975. This book, though published in 1975, nevertheless provides an analysis of the Communist system as it was implemented in North Korea, including discussion of issues such as government structure, mass mobilization campaigns, economic development strategies, and North Korea's maneuvering between the Soviet Union and China.

Alexandra Kura, ed., *Rogue Countries: Background and Current Issues*, Appendix I. Huntingdon, NY: Nova Science, 2001. This is a volume of essays on various countries viewed as "rogues," including North Korea, considering the danger they pose to the rest of the world as a result of issues such as nuclear weapons and other weapons of mass destruction.

Andrei Lankov, *From Stalin to Kim Il Sung.* London: Hurst, 2002. This well-researched and recently published book focuses on the history of North Korea from the end of World War II to 1956, when opponents of Kim Il Sung staged the only known challenge to his regime.

Koon Woo Nam, *The North Korean Communist Leadership, 1945–1965.* Tuscaloosa: University of Alabama Press, 1974. This book traces the Communist influence on North Korea, from the time of Japanese occupation of Korea prior to the formation of North Korea to the early decades of the regime of Kim Il Sung.

Don Oberdorfer, *The Two Koreas.* New York: Basic Books, 2001. This is a readable history of modern North Korea from the time of its creation until the year 2000, which marked the first summit between the two Korean leaders.

Han S. Park, *North Korea, The Politics of Unconventional Wisdom.* Boulder, CO: Lynne Rienner, 2002. This is a study of the *Juche* political philosophy as it has developed in North Korea under the leadership of Kim Il Sung by a leading expert on the topic.

Andrea Matles Savada, ed., *North Korea, A Country Study.* Washington, DC: Library of Congress, 1994. This is a Library of Congress study and report on North Korea, providing a good overview of its history, society, economy, government, military, and foreign policy.

Chong-Sik and Se-He Yoo, eds., *North Korea in Transition.* Berkeley: University of California Press, 1991. This book, although published in 1991, contains several essays on topics relevant today, such as the changes brought by the collapse of the Soviet Union and North Korea's search for a national identity.

Geoff Simons, *Korea: The Search for Sovereignty.* New York: St. Martin's, 1995. This is a valuable history of North Korea written by a freelance author covering early Korean history as well as the development of modern North Korea following the Korean War.

Hazel Smith et al., eds., *North Korea in the New World Order.* New York: St. Martin's, 1996. A collection of essays by different authors, written in a scholarly manner, this book addresses issues facing modern North Korea, such as economic reform, the role of *Juche*, and U.S. policy toward the country.

Periodicals

Arms Control Today, "Progress and Challenges in Denuclearizing North Korea," May 2002.

Associated Press, "North Korea's Official Radio Backs Off Nuke Report," November 15, 2002.

Paul Chamberlin, "A Realistic U.S. Policy," *World & I*, January 2003.

Erik Eckholm, "North Korea Presses Demand for Direct Talks with U.S.," *New York Times*, January 31, 2003.

Daniel Goodkind and Loraine West, "The North Korean Famine and Its Demographic Impact," *Population and Development Review*, June 2001.

Michael R. Gordon and Felicity Barringer, "North Korea Wants Arms and More Aid from U.S.," *New York Times*, February 12, 2003.

Nicolette Jackson and Sean Healy, "Desperate Escape: The Backbreaking Work of North Korean Women," *New Internationalist*, September 2002.

Paul Kerr, "U.S. Sends Conflicting Signals on North Korea," *Arms Control Today*, September 2002.

Yongho Kim, "North Korea's Use of Terror and Coercive Diplomacy: Looking for Their Circumstantial Variants," *Korean Journal of Defense Analysis*, Spring 2002.

Tae-Hwan Kwak and Seung-Ho Joo, "The Korean Peace Process: Problems and Prospects After the Summit," *World Affairs*, Fall 2002.

Marc Lerner, "North Korea Weapons a 'Nuclear Nightmare,'" *Washington Times*, January 17, 2003.

John J. Lumpkin, "U.S. Assesses North Korea's Military," Associated Press, January 9, 2003.

Donald Macintyre, "Light from the North?" *Time International*, August 19, 2002.

Johanna McGeary, "Look Who's Got the Bomb," *Time*, October 28, 2002.

Oil Daily, "N. Korea Blames Breach on U.S.," November 22, 2002.

Time, "How Dangerous Is North Korea?" January 13, 2003.

Notra Trulock, "North Korea's Nuclear Threat," *Insight on the News*, May 20, 2002.

United Press International, "N. Korea Blasts U.S. Nuclear Strategy," March 13, 2002.

Bryan Walsh, "Dead Wrong?" *Time International*, November 23, 2002.

Kathryn Weathersby, "The Korean War Revisited," *Wilson Quarterly*, Summer 1999.

Internet Sources
John R. Bolton, speech in Seoul, South Korea, August 29,

2002. Office of International Information Programs, U.S. Department of State. http://usinfo.state.gov.

George W. Bush, "President's State of the Union Address," Washington, DC, January 29, 2002. www.whitehouse.gov.

———, "The National Security Strategy of the United States," report to Congress, September 20, 2002. www.whitehouse. gov.

Cable News Network, "Tenet: North Korea Has Ballistic Missile Capable of Hitting U.S.," February 12, 2003. www.cnn.com.

Joseph Hong, "Korean Studies," University of California at Berkeley. http://socrates.berkeley.edu.

Gaurav Kampani et al., "Overview of North Korea's Ballistic Missile Program," Center for Nonproliferation Studies, Monterey Institute of International Studies, 2002. http://cns.miis.edu.

Sato Katsumi, "Why North Korea Kidnapped Japanese Citizens," Modern Korea Institute. www.bekkoame.ne.jp.

Korea Web Weekly, "July 10 Hwang Jang Yop Press Conference." www.kimsoft.com.

Radio Veritas Asia, "Summit Agreement Between North and South Korea." www.catholic.org.

Lee Wha Rang, "N. Korea Nuclear Arsenal," Federation of American Scientists. www.kimsoft.com.

U.S. Department of State, "Democratic People's Republic of Korea, Country Reports on Human Rights Practices—2001," March 4, 2002. www.state.gov.

Website
Office of International Information Programs, U.S. Department of State (http://usinfo.state.gov). The Office of International Information Programs (IIP) is the principal international communications service for the foreign affairs community. The website contains links to speeches by government officials, documents, and policy papers as well as links to other websites.

Index

Picture Credits

About the Author

Debra A. Miller is a writer and lawyer with an interest in current events and history. She began her law career in Washington, D.C., where she worked on legislative, policy, and legal matters in government, public interest, and private law firm positions. She now lives with her husband in Encinitas, California. She has written and edited numerous publications for legal publishers, as well as books and anthologies on historical and political topics.